Coming Out Restored

Struggles With Self and Sexuality Made New

Tiffany Sullivan

Contents

Dedication	v
Introduction	ix
1. Into the Woods and Out of the Closet	1
2. Sprouting	22
3. Dry Lands	39
4. Fenceless Gardens	57
5. Uprooted	74
6. Where the Moss Grows	88
7. A Wolf in Sheep's Clothing	103
8. Watering Weeds	118
9. Tree Stumps	133
10. Seeing Sunflowers	149
Conclusion	165
Notes	167
Acknowledgments	171

Copyright © 2024 by Tiffany Sullivan *Coming Out Restored*.

All rights reserved. No part of this publication may be reproduced, distributed, or transmitted in any form or by any means, without prior written permission.

Printed in the United States of America

First Edition

All Scripture quotations, unless otherwise indicated, are taken from the Holy Bible, New International Version®, NIV®. Copyright ©1973, 1978, 1984, 2011 by Biblica, Inc.™ Used by permission of Zondervan. All rights reserved worldwide. www.zondervan.com The "NIV" and "New International Version" are trademarks registered in the United States Patent and Trademark Office by Biblica, Inc.™

Scripture quotations are from The ESV® Bible (The Holy Bible, English Standard Version®), © 2001 by Crossway, a publishing ministry of Good News Publishers. Used by permission. All rights reserved.

Scripture quotations marked NLT are taken from the *Holy Bible*, New Living Translation, Copyright © 1996, 2004, 2015 by Tyndale House Foundation. Used by permission of Tyndale House Publishers, Inc., Carol Stream, Illinois 60188. All rights reserved.

Scripture quotations marked NKJV taken from the New King James Version®. Copyright © 1982 by Thomas Nelson. Used by permission. All rights reserved.

ISBN-13: 979-8-3305-6650-1 (print)

ISBN-13: 979-8-3305-6651-8 (ebook)

Dedication

This book is written for the lost, the skeptic, and the praying loved one.

A Letter to You, Who Has Walked Away From God.

Hi,

It's so nice to meet you. I pray someday we will cross paths so I can see face-to-face the person I've been praying for and hear word-for-word the details of your life that's so uniquely and beautifully woven into God's grand story. I wholeheartedly believe that God has placed this book in your hands intentionally, not because the story I have to tell is more special than the next but because He wants you to know just how deeply He adores you. I know firsthand what it feels like to be lost and far from God. I remember the days I thought He had abandoned me. More than that, I know what it feels like to know without a doubt that God never left me. I understand now what it looks like to live life on the other side of grace and mercy where the love of God is so intense that I can confidently say nothing on this earth compares to. I pray this over your life. Your life was no mistake. You were created for a purpose that far exceeds what meets the eye. And I pray you come to know the Savior in such a deeply intimate way that you realize, just as I have, that nothing in the world comes close to choosing life God's way. You are so loved by your Creator who made you in His perfect image. May He restore whatever in your life that's been broken. May He redeem all that the enemy has been using to destroy you. And may you come to experience God in a supernatural way.

A Letter to You, Who isn't Sure What to Think of Christ.

Hi,

I feel honored that this book has landed in your lap. It is no coincidence. I love you, I've been praying for you, and I hope to meet you in person. I would love to hear your curiosities and skepticism about following Jesus. I surely don't have all the answers, but I would love to lend a listening ear. Thank you for wanting to hear my story. My prayer is that more than the story I have to tell about how God has moved in my life, that scripture would jump off these pages and into your heart. I pray you encounter the love of God in such a real way that some of your questions and doubts are resolved. May God reveal Himself and His good plan to you. My one piece of advice, if you're open to it, is don't let a limit of what you believe God can or cannot do settle in your heart. Abandon your decisiveness of who you think you are and ask God, who you actually are. With that, I hope you begin to see that you were without a doubt created in the image of God Almighty for such a time as this. And then, I hope you come to understand just how incredible that truth is. As you continue this journey of discovering truth, I pray for the peace that surpasses all understanding to cover you.

A Letter to You, the Loved One Who is Praying for Change.

Hi,

Gosh, I want to hug you. If it weren't for people like you who prayed me through the darkest seasons of my life, I truly don't know where I would be. At the time, I didn't want the prayers. In fact, I wanted the opposite. I wanted those people to love me in the way I thought they should love me – in full acceptance of the life I was choosing. I thought their prayers represented hate and for that I harbored a lot of resentment. I am so grateful that those who chose to pray for me daily, didn't stop. I'm glad that they never championed me with statements of validation but rather chose to pray and wait. I'm glad they continued praying for me even when they felt their prayers weren't being heard. I am filled with joy knowing I am the product of praying loved ones. My first encouragement to you - don't stop praying. There is a spiritual battle and you are called to be a part of God's army. Lean on God to Ephesians 6:10-18 your way through this. I pray God gives you peace and strength to continue standing in Truth against a world that wants you to believe a lie that your prayers are not loving. My second encouragement to you – ask your trusted community to pray with you and for you. So many people went to war for me in prayer because my parents were faithful to ask. As you ask for your community to partner with you in prayer, know that I am praying alongside you. May your loved one know he or she is fearfully and wonderfully made in the perfect image of God.

Introduction

I've had this book on my heart for years but, quite frankly, wasn't sure where to start. I knew the portion of my testimony that includes dating another woman would likely catch a lot of attention I wasn't ready to face. When I came out with my relationship, I received a variety of reactions and felt the impact of others' changed opinions of me. Likewise, I imagine there will be a variety of reactions and opinions regarding this kind of "coming out," especially in a public manner. Some people may be completely off-put by my openness and faith, seeing this book as an attack. Others may be skeptical of my intentions. These types of responses have held me captive in fear, concerned more about what others think than others may receive. Over the last few years, I have heard more stories of people within the church and those who used to be part of the church facing similar temptations and struggles as I have. I finally came to terms with the fact that keeping this story to myself was selfish. I've taken the last several months to write out what God has laid on my heart prayerfully. My purpose in telling this story is, first and foremost, an act of worship to God

Introduction

for what He's done and what He's doing. Secondly, I pray that at least one person is touched by reading this story. Regardless of whether you struggle with sexual identity or some other issue with yourself, I hope God touches you throughout these pages. His will be done.

Although several chapters involve details of that specific season in my life, I want to be clear that being in a homosexual relationship was never the central issue. The sin of self has always been the issue – self-image, self-righteousness, self-hate, and self-sufficiency, to name a few. I haven't always struggled with my sexual identity. In fact, I didn't know if I should even identify as a lesbian when I dated another woman. The label never resonated with me. What resonated with me was an intense longing to love and be loved in the way I had dreamed of since childhood. With dreams of a fairy tale life, finding my one true love was my heart's greatest desire. I wanted a love story worth shouting from the rooftops. In the midst of my longing to encounter such deep affection, I simultaneously believed I was unworthy of such love, and for that, I hated myself. What I didn't see at the time was that I actually needed to encounter a love that even fairy tales couldn't compete with. I needed the only Love capable of filling the gaps I so desperately tried to fill myself. I needed the Greatest Love of all – Jesus Christ.

Maybe you can relate to my story in some ways. Whether you understand struggles with sexuality or self, I believe we've all experienced a search for something to provide us with wholeness, worth, or purpose. Some of us more intensely than others. If you are a believer in Christ, once considered yourself a believer, or are a skeptic, I hope you see the evidence that God is speaking to you and constantly providing opportunities for you to experience His love firsthand. I don't consider myself to have all the answers, and I'm certainly not a theologian.

Introduction

What I am is a changed person who wants to encourage you to seek answers to the questions you have and to open your heart to what God wants to do with those questions.

As honored and blessed as I am that you have chosen to read this book, I want you to know nothing on these pages compares to encountering God the Father, Jesus, and the Holy Spirit for yourself. I encourage you to open the Bible, read His Word, and talk to Him. Welcome Him into your circumstances as they currently are. Be honest about your doubts, fears, and any anger you feel. Then ask Him (and you can qualify your request with "if you're real") to reveal Himself to you. What's the worst that could happen?

I would never suggest that anyone make the choices I did, and at the same time, I'm incredibly grateful to have walked through some very dark seasons. In every struggle, God has granted me the opportunity to witness the power and freedom only He offers. I am convinced *there is no greater love* than the Lover of my soul. I know without a doubt that nothing on this earth compares to life with Him. By God's grace and mercy, a life destined for destruction has been redeemed. By the power and freedom of Christ's sacrifice on the cross, this is my coming out story. From death to life, I am restored.

Chapter 1

Into the Woods and Out of the Closet

"Mom, I have something to tell you and Dad," I stammered through the phone. There was a brief silence, followed by my mom's response.

A slow "...okay..."

Her response cut like a knife. As my mom went to get my dad, I took a deep breath and thought, *"Thank God I had those drinks ahead of time. There's no way I could do this sober".*

I was glad to have the liquid courage to tell my parents something that was sure to rock their world. My dad got on the phone, and my mom asked what I had to say to them. "You know my best friend? She's not just a friend. I'm dating her." I didn't know how to soften the blow of revealing a secret I had kept for two years.

"What?"

My mom's voice was faint. The world we once knew as a family now felt like a distant memory.

I can't remember what else my mom said, and quite frankly, considering my liquor-induced state, I remember it all a little blurry. She seemed rushed to get off the phone, and I'm pretty sure my dad didn't have much to say either.

There was no "I love you" to end the call. Just a quick "goodbye." Truthfully, I figured it was the last goodbye I would hear from my parents for a while. I had planned for this. I knew they would be caught off guard since they only knew me as my previous boy-crazy self. To my surprise, my mom called back about twenty minutes later.

I barely hit the answer button before my mom blurted, "What happened?"

Confused, I asked, "What do you mean?"

She went through the list of possible causes.

Disoriented, she wondered how the daughter, who used to overshare about the guys she dated and wanted to marry, now had a girlfriend. Our previous discussions of me and her future son-in-law were suddenly trivial.

"Did *we* do something wrong?" Her mom guilt sank in.

"Mom, it's not about you guys. I fell in love with her." I nearly choked on my words. I knew telling my parents I had a girlfriend was enough, but telling them I loved her would surely disorient them.

Somewhere in our initial conversations, I remember my dad asking if I was going to marry her. I thought it was a rather pointed question, considering they just found out I was dating her. The question made my skin itch. I wasn't sure what to say and couldn't answer directly. The truth is that we had been dating for two years already, and the topic of marriage had come up between us. I knew I couldn't keep our relationship a secret much longer if marriage was on the table. It was the right thing to do by her to tell my parents. I couldn't continue to keep us so hidden from the world. Surely, it was the right thing for me as well, or at least, that's what I was telling myself. I knew she made me happy, and I made her happy. I couldn't picture my life without her, so I thought this was the right thing to do.

As the days and weeks passed from what I like to call "D-Day" (a.k.a. "Drop the biggest bomb my parents had ever heard Day"), the finality of my decision began to sink in.

It was the right thing to do...right?

And by right thing, I mean to come clean after two years of lying to my family and move my relationship with her forward so we could start planning the future.

It had to have been the right thing to do.

One thing was for sure. There was no turning back. It was set in stone who I was. Lesbian. Or was it Bisexual? I wasn't certain and didn't particularly enjoy having a label for my sexuality. Either way, I knew I could no longer consider myself straight.

The ease of keeping this major secret for two years came on the tail of a major shift in my life. About 2.5 years prior, I packed a car full of my belongings for a job interview as a wilderness counselor for troubled youth. I took the job 2,000 miles away in the woods of a town most Floridians have never heard of. My contact with the outside world for those years was minimal. The physical distance between my parents and me was a catalyst that made hiding my new reality quite smooth. It was easy to forget I hadn't told them yet because I lived in a safe little bubble of people who loved and accepted me as I was. I felt welcomed, comfortable, and validated in my relationship.

I was protected by the little bubble I had found in the woods. I was in love—so in love—with her. She was my world. What else could I want? I convinced myself I didn't need a deep relationship with my parents (if it came to that) because I had everything I ever wanted. I was everything I wanted to be. I wanted to be somebody worthy of great love and somebody who could reciprocate that great love.

Loving her became my identity.

We were inseparable, always agreed, and made the perfect team. I was sure a life without her was not worth living. So, when I finally told my parents, it didn't matter that their world appeared to be ending. I had my world, and that was all that mattered.

Marked by Moments

Life is complex, and we humans are complex. Because of that, each of us experiences life in a unique way.

Where and when we were born, the beliefs and values we were raised around or picked up along the way, our genetic makeup, our demeanor, etc., each make us unique individuals. Two people could come from very similar situations, but because one aspect about them is slightly different, their worldviews are completely different. When people have different worldviews, similar situations two people go through are likely to have a unique impact on each person.

No matter how different or similar we are, monumental moments in life can throw us off a path we once believed we were on. Sometimes, the shift in trajectory is deemed good, sometimes bad. Regardless, we tend to hold these big life happenings as markers of who we are.

I've had many life-defining moments. One day in elementary school, my best friend said she was prettier than me. Soon after, a couple of girls in my ballet class pointed out that my legs were chubbier than theirs. In another instance, I was running in a bathing suit with a friend when she pointed out that my legs were jiggling.

These early life moments told me:

1. My body was the most important part of me.

2. I was not enough because several people were prettier and thinner than me.
3. My purpose was to improve my physical appearance in order to increase my value.

Those moments marked me as insufficient and inferior. Perhaps you can relate. Perhaps your life was marked by the abuse you experienced as a child or as an adult. Maybe your life-defining moments surround someone verbally attacking you. You may have been told you weren't smart enough, creative enough, or successful enough.

On the other hand, maybe you experienced a great deal of praise for one reason or another, and that verbal affirmation solidified the "you" you must maintain. All of these experiences, whether positive or negative, write something on our hearts and in our minds about who we are. These experiences tell us there is a piece of us that can never be changed or a piece of us that is only worthy if it remains. These life markers either drive us into repeating the patterns set in motion for us or detour us in the opposite direction. Regardless, life moments like these become a part of who we are. We need to ask ourselves whether our experiences are truly worthy of so much power over us. Should these significant moments actually have the power to define us? No matter the power over us, it is understandable why we would be so affected by our experiences. It is okay for big moments to change us forever. It is normal for us to walk through life encountering deeply impactful moments along the way.

The Bible talks about the pain we feel in our earthly lives and compares it to childbirth (Romans 8:22 ESV). Childbirth, described by many women as the most physical pain they have ever known, is a graphic comparison. I personally happened to think I was on the verge of death during labor. So, when comparing our earthly lives to one of the most physically painful and grueling experiences I've known, it doesn't surprise me that we can be so affected by what happens in our lives. The things we go through can be the most excruciating experiences and, rightfully so, become extremely powerful in how we live our lives. However, the real power lies in the purpose of the pain. The imagery of life being like childbirth implies that the inevitable pain we will face on earth has a purpose of new birth. The truth is God desires to turn the pain we experience into something brand new.

> "Praise be to the God and Father of our Lord Jesus Christ! In his great mercy he has given us new birth into a living hope through the resurrection of Jesus Christ from the dead."
>
> — 1 Peter 1:3 ESV

When we are in the midst of a major shift in life, especially one that hurts, it's nearly impossible to see the benefit of "new birth" to come. I won't sit here and pretend that even today, when I am going through something difficult, my first instinct is to think of anything but the worst-case scenario. I would be lying if I said it was in my nature to look forward to what will come out of my pain. Sure, I look forward to the end of suffering, but considering my pain to be beneficial in the end is still foreign to me. Looking outside myself is the only way I am able to see hope for the future when I am suffering. Recognizing that there is a bigger, grander story than mine helps put what is to come into perspective. It is so much easier said than done but what if that is how we lived day-to-day? What would it look like if our histories and experiences merely tell a portion of the story in a magnificent eternal story? When we are able to shift our perspectives externally to the impact our stories have on the lives around us, something great happens.

The Bible tells us in Colossians 1:16, "For in him all things were created: things in heaven and on earth, visible and invisible, whether thrones or powers or rulers or authorities; all things have been created through him and for him." ALL things...that includes you and me. That includes all of the details about us. That includes everything and everyone in the Universe. We were created through Him and for Him.

Furthermore, we are promised completeness through Christ. Colossians 2:10 explains that those who believe in Christ "have been brought to fullness." That means that if you have put your faith in Christ, you are made complete. There is nothing missing about you or your story because Christ completes it. Nothing about your past, present, or future can make you less or make you more because Christ completes you.

I don't know about you, but this truth offers me so much hope and relief. I feel hopeful that the messy parts of me don't get to hold so much power. I feel relief that the parts of me that are clean aren't a standard I always have to live up to. There is a special freedom in knowing Christ is the One who brings us to fullness.

> "And we know that in all things God works for the good of those who love him."
>
> — Romans 8:28

What the World Says About Who We Are

It's no secret the world values labels. The topic of identity has become a quite complicated focus of society. There's an unspoken pressure to fit in and, at the same time, stand out.

The expectation of accepting everyone as they are comes without saying. The term "identity" has been around for a long time. I find it interesting that the origin of its meaning is "sameness, oneness, state of being the same."[1] Conversely, culture today primarily seems to view identity as fluid and something that may change from day to day or even minute by minute. A person's identity is now driven by feelings and what happens to the person rather than the truth of who he or she is. It's less about "oneness" and more about a variety of characteristics that make up the person.

Personal identity and social identity are often the drivers of discussion when deciding who a person is. Personal identity is what makes the person unique via emotions, physical features, intellect, habits, and memory. Social identity is essentially how the person fits into society, such as socioeconomic status, age, race, religion, sexual orientation, nationality, etc. Although every aspect that describes personal and social identity can define a person, I would argue that this does not reflect true identity. If identity means sameness, wouldn't your unique attributes and I be insignificant in the context of true identity? Wouldn't the origin and intention of our creation hold more weight than anything else? The phrase "my truth" engraved on recent generations begs to let fate and feelings define the person. "My truth" contradicts the definition of "truth," which is defined as "the body of real things, events, and facts (actuality) or the state of being the case (fact)."[2] My truth is based on personal beliefs and emotions instead of facts.

Another common phrase tossed around, as a matter of fact, is "This is who I am." The author of *Holy Sexuality*, Christopher Yuan, recalled a classmate in seminary who, upon leaving his wife and coming out gay, claimed, "This is who I am." His confidence in the statement was used to justify his decision to leave his family to "live his truth." In his book,

Christopher shares his personal testimony of Christ calling him out of a life marked by selling drugs, imprisonment, homosexuality, and a diagnosis of HIV is powerful. Instead of Christopher settling with "this is who I am," his heart opened to the transformative power of the Gospel. His heart became open to understanding who he always was outside of the drugs, criminal record, homosexuality, and HIV.[3]

If you can relate to Christopher's classmate and believe you are who you are and cannot change, I understand. When a part of us feels inherent, it is difficult to see ourselves without that piece of us. It's not unusual to credit certain traits as permanent and unwavering. Medical diagnoses, for example, sometimes tell us what diseases we must permanently label ourselves with. Psychological evaluations cause us to identify with our mental and emotional distinctions, and family history indicates the probability of how we will turn out. Identifying ourselves with the aspects of our lives that make us unique is common. We even have a tendency to identify with our personality traits. Our sense of humor is considered to be as steadfast as the freckles on our faces. Our pessimistic nature is thought to be unchanging, like our blood type. The truth is, some of these things about us will never change. We may always have that medical or mental health diagnosis. We may end up struggling with the same issues we've seen in our family. The problem is, with these labels, we often have difficulty seeing past what we have accepted as ours. The chance for something different or something more dissipates because we've accepted ourselves as "This is who I am."

Again, I get it. This has been part of my story. I claimed negativity as my natural state of being. My struggle with depression, self-harm, and an eating disorder became who I was over time as my attempts at being something different continued to fail. I was given different psychological diagnoses, prescribed a variety of medications, and attempted several different therapeutic approaches. After what seemed like unanswered prayer after unanswered prayer and multiple failed therapeutic interventions, I believed these things I struggled with were inalterable aspects of my identity. I assumed I would forever identify as a self-harming person with depression and an eating disorder. I reduced my identity to the things in my life that felt natural and permanent. I genuinely thought I could not change. I presume my belief that I could not change, in part, caused me to remain stuck in an identity that caused immense harm to myself and others.

Settling in an identity that wasn't meant to be mine became missed opportunities to respond in a way that reflected the truth of who I am – freed by Christ. Thank God, my story didn't end there.

How We are Wired

Relationships are at the core of our existence and the cause and effect of our choices. How we connect with ourselves and relate to the people and the world around us is central to how and why we live. We were wired *to love* and *to be known*. The intimacy we encounter when we are both loved and known simultaneously meets an emotional need in a way nothing else in life can. Authentic relationships are life-giving.

Our need to be known is partnered closely with our love need. We were created for a deep and genuine connection with God and others. Love, in its purest form, requires being truly known in relationships. This means we have security in being accepted for who we truly are. This also means accepting and loving others in the same way. Without being known, any love we experience is shallow and conditional. To experience authentic love in any relationship, there must be the depth of *knowing* each other. Tim Keller says it well:

> "To be loved but not known is comforting but superficial. To be known and not loved is our greatest fear. But to be fully known and truly loved is, well, a lot like being loved by God. It is what we need more than anything. It liberates us from pretense, humbles us out of our self-righteousness, and fortifies us for any difficulty life can throw at us."[4]

Being known in love is to experience intimacy. Intimacy, both protective and freeing, is necessary for us to experience harmony in life. We are made to connect deeply with others. When we meet and respond to this need appropriately, our health is positively impacted. In fact, our brain function is affected by fulfilled emotional needs. In the book *The Perfect You*, Dr. Caroline Leaf sheds light on how positive feelings like peacefulness and self-confidence activate a part of our brain. The corpus striatum is stimulated by these types of feelings as reinforcements. If we do not feel safe, that part of the brain does not engage. Essentially, within our innate wiring for love, certain parts of our brain remain stagnant unless we are experiencing the feelings that correspond with love.[5] Like stagnant water, issues arise when the brain is left unused at its greatest potential.

Unsurprisingly, the brain is intended to be activated rather than remain idle. In attempts to function fully, the brain will compensate, when given the opportunity, with counterfeit "good feelings" signaled by a variety of addictive substances. Cocaine and the typical unhealthy American diet are counterfeits that impact the corpus striatum in similar ways. The momentary good feeling a person experiences when using addictive drugs or eating a dopamine-filled, sugary treat becomes the reason to reuse or indulge in the substance again. It's the feeling the addict chases, not the substance. Dr. Leaf shares that the most powerful tool to overcome addiction is the choice to overcome it.[6] Of course, there is so much that goes into addiction and brain function, but the key thing to consider is that our brains were created to respond to positive "love" feelings, and we will do what it takes to meet that need even when it means choosing an unhealthy means of doing so. When we have chosen unhealthy means to meet our love needs, it requires choice at the forefront to combat our destructive proclivities. In relating this to my own experience with depression, self-harm, and an eating disorder, until I truly made the choice to live differently, I remained stuck in a cycle. Before I felt any sense of freedom from mental illnesses, I made a conscious effort to break up the pattern I was in. To be clear, this was not an overnight change. It took years to believe it was possible to become healthy before I saw the choices I had control over. Then, it required practice to choose not to engage in my eating disorder and self-harm. The most important thing to note is before I was able to make the choice to practice something different, I began to see love differently than I had before. Ultimately, there was a shift in how I experienced true love. Just as the Bible promises, I began to *believe* the love God has for me (1 John 4:16 ESV).

There is no greater love we can experience in this life than the love of God. Even the most intimate and sincerest relationship we build with another person cannot compare. The most magnificent aspect of God's love for us is that He already knows us completely; therefore, His love is perfect from the get-go. He doesn't need to wait for us to tell Him our deepest, darkest secrets to love us; He already knows. He created us and loves us fully. The only caveat is that we must accept His love to live in it. With no requirement from us other than receiving His gift of love, we are granted the only perfect love that exists. Nothing else compares to the love of God, and nothing can separate us from His good and perfect love when we accept it.

> "No power in the sky above or in the earth below—indeed, nothing in all creation will ever be able to separate us from the love of God that is revealed in Christ Jesus our Lord."
>
> — Romans 8:39 NLT

Driven by Fear

So if we have this free gift of perfect love, why do we struggle to understand who we truly are? Why is it difficult to comprehend and live on the truth that we are made complete (Colossians 2:10 NKJV) and free in Christ (John 8:36 NKJV)? The answer is that we live in a fallen world. When sin entered the world, fear followed suit. Before the fall, Adam and Eve "were both naked but felt no shame" (Genesis 2:25 NKJV). God had instructed Adam not to eat from the Tree of Knowledge of Good and Evil (Genesis 2:17) because doing so would lead to death. The devil disguised himself as a snake and asked Eve if God *really* said they must not eat from *any* tree in the garden (Genesis 3:1). Notice the qualifiers "really" and "any" were used intentionally to push back on what Eve already knew to be true. Satan wanted her to second-guess what she already knew. Eve knew the answer and relayed what she knew: that they were not to eat from the tree in the middle of the garden because if they did, they would die (Genesis 3:2-3). Satan continued his lies and said eating the fruit would not lead to death. He said that God knew if they ate the fruit, their eyes would be opened, so they would be like God. Eve began to believe the devil's deception and to desire the wisdom she could gain from eating the fruit (Genesis 3:6 NKJV). When Eve decided to eat the fruit and share it with Adam, she was operating out of the fear that they were missing out on something. How often do we do that in life? We see something we haven't had before and feel like we are missing out. The qualifiers "really" and "any" convince us our desires aren't *that bad*.

We're on a tight budget, but seeing the newest kitchen gadget that so-and-so claimed changed her life... "You know, that appliance *really* would cook food faster."

Our closet is overflowing with clothes, and the style changes, and we think, "I need more clothes; I don't have *any*thing to wear."

The doctor tells us our health is at risk because we are overweight, but when we are offered a dessert at work, we can't resist because "One dessert doesn't *really* matter." Besides, saying "no" would be rude.

Sometimes, what is at stake is more serious, but we qualify our decision with "just this once" or "it's only hurting me." You see, the devil's ways are conniving. He wants to create doubt in who we are and what we have. He wants us to live in fear that something good is being withheld from us. He wants us to believe that one decision *really* won't make *any* difference in the scheme of things. He knows that if we can make our decisions based on fear disguised as missing out, he can eventually win us over.

The truth is we aren't missing out on anything when we live in the presence of God. With Him, we already have everything we need. Adam and Eve had everything they needed. God had granted them full access to every other tree in the garden and restricted the tree of knowledge of good and evil out of protection. The devil knew that if he could plant fear in

Adam and Eve's minds that they were missing out, he could ultimately win them over to sin. What was the result of their decision to eat the fruit? It was not "good" as they had anticipated. They became aware of their nakedness and were afraid (Genesis 3:10 ESV). When we make decisions rooted in fear, the outcome is not fulfilling. Sometimes, the outcome of one decision made out of fear is immediately devastating. Most often, there is a buildup of one decision based on fear after another that leads to something excruciating.

When I look back at my relationship with another woman, I see the progression of my decisions. I recognize that I was afraid of being alone. I am aware that I rationalized my care for her and the success of our relationship as the right relationship for me. I was afraid no one else would compare. What I also see is how the progression of my decisions hurt not only her and me but also other people in our lives. Before the romance, I remember feeling like we were meant to be in each other's lives. To this day, I believe that to be the case. Now I know that my fear of missing out led me to a relationship Satan wanted me to see as good. I allowed a perverse and false version of love to disrupt the genuine and holy love intended for that friendship. Ironically, my decision to enter into a romantic relationship with her was like Eve eating the fruit. It left me bare and feeling more fear than I had initially.

Driven by Love

> "God is love, and all who live in love live in God, and God lives in them. And as we live in God, our love grows more perfect. So we will not be afraid on the day of judgment, but we can face him with confidence because we live like Jesus here in this world. Such love has no fear, because perfect love

expels all fear. If we are afraid, it is for fear of punishment, and this shows that we have not fully experienced His perfect love."

— 1 John 4:16-18 NLT

This past year, I received counseling from a wonderful Christian woman whose approach to counseling is based on restoring relationships with God the Father. Most of us have "father wounds" that we have carried from our childhood into relationships throughout our lives. Regardless of how wonderful our fathers were or weren't, their humanity impacted us at one point or another. I didn't realize that I had father wounds that needed healing. Like every father, mine was not perfect, but he was a good dad. I didn't think much about the possibility that I still had wounds that needed healing. Through the counseling, I realized that the wounds I felt from childhood surrounded missed expectations. We uncovered the perfect expectations I had of my father that he was not able to live up to. I felt guilty for being sad about what I saw as missing in our relationship. I needed healing from my guilt and shame and forgiveness for holding my father to unachievable standards. My missed expectations transpired in how I viewed God, and the therapy I received exposed my misunderstanding of God, the only perfect Father.

After my wounds were exposed, healing began. I accepted my father's humanity and released my expectations to God. I allowed God's good and perfect love to envelop my tender heart. I repented of the ways I unintentionally held my father's shortcomings over his head. I accepted God's perfect fatherly love. Once this happened, I experienced the sweetest moment with my heavenly Father. In my time alone with Him, I felt the tangible, perfect love of a father that my heart had always craved. I felt my flesh of guilt, shame, and inadequacies wash away as I sat in His presence. I felt the comfort of His strength and assurance like a hand resting atop my left shoulder. It was as if my heart was getting a hug I had always craved.

What wounds did you experience growing up that only the perfect Father can heal? Perhaps nothing bad happened but your heart still feels something amiss. Maybe your childhood, like mine, was good, but there's a yearning that nothing in life seems to fulfill. Maybe you know your wounds, but you don't know where to start. If you have difficulty seeing God as a good and perfect Father, chances are your heart has wounds that need healing.

I'm still learning to accept human error in relationships, but I have experienced the healing work of God the Father. The Perfect Father, the Giver of Life and Sovereign Protector, enables us to live in love. We can feel sad when someone does not live up to our expectations without harboring bitterness or guilt. We can allow ourselves to be disappointed without trying to force change. We can release relationships to the Lord and allow His perfect love to fill the gaps. In turn, allowing God's love to fill the empty spaces produces a version of us that is more loving and has purer motives. We see the world in a different light. We recognize the pain in others and see that hope is needed now more than ever. Our decisions begin to fall in line with love instead of fear. We find ourselves less offended and more compassionate. We make fewer attempts to control because we realize our control causes more hurt in the end. We see the power that love holds and enjoy the peace it brings.

Part Spirit, Part Flesh

We won't do life perfectly, navigate relationships with others perfectly, or execute our relationships with ourselves perfectly.

We are part spirit and part flesh, and the two are often at odds. Marrying the two so our choices remain as consistent and healthy as possible requires a work of God.

Our spirit is the essence of who we are deep down. It's the part of us that knows there is more to this life and doesn't find satisfaction in the superficial motives of this world. Our spirit beckons us to find meaning and peace when the world around us is loud, demanding, and chaotic. Our spirit is what continues after our body has disintegrated. It connects us to eternity.

On the contrary, our flesh is the tangible shell of our body and is evident in our fleeting desires. Our flesh is in the short term. Our flesh leads us to find temporary fixes and momentary satisfactions. Our flesh is incapable of deeper meaning because it is decaying daily. The destination of our flesh is the ground. It is unavoidable, but because we are both spirit and part flesh, our flesh will always want to find meaning in the temporary.

With our spirit set on eternity but our mind focused on the present life, our day-to-day functioning can become quite tumultuous. It is difficult to ignore the troubles and triumphs of now and focus solely on what is ahead. The war we face each day to live in the present but with an eternal perspective is incredibly difficult and sometimes feels impossible.

I remember the days I begged and pleaded with God to take my depression away. I knew that eternity called me to a more peaceful state of mind, but my flesh wouldn't allow it, no matter what I tried. None of it worked: the pills, the therapy, the psychologists, the pastoral counseling. What I failed to accept was that my attempts to "heal" were based out of fear. I was afraid that if I allowed God to really work on me and clean me of the junk that was keeping me depressed, I would be left bare. I identified with my depression for so long that I believed I would be giving up a part of myself if I put in the spiritual work that was needed. The truth is I would have been giving up part of me, my flesh. I was scared because I knew I would be losing something familiar to me and would be left with the scars of my past. I wanted nothing more than to snap my fingers for it to be gone as if it had never happened. I wanted the memories of hating myself to disappear. Essentially, I wanted to be a completely new person. The irony is that I was already a new person but wasn't living as if I were. I was missing the key to living differently - living for eternity by the power of the Holy Spirit.

> "So I say, walk by the Spirit, and you will not gratify the desires of the flesh. For the flesh desires what is contrary to the Spirit, and the Spirit what is contrary to the flesh. They are in conflict with each other so that you are not able to do whatever you want without clashing. But if you are led by the Spirit, you are not under the law ."
>
> — Galatians 5:16-18

We can learn a lot from Paul in the Bible. He understood the war mankind faces between spirit and flesh and spent much of his ministry pointing believers to the key ingredient to winning the battle – by *living in the Spirit*. He recognized our frailty and admitted that he, too, was weak (2 Corinthians 12:7). Paul even boasted about his weakness because he knew that the power of God was perfected in it (2 Corinthians 11:30). Paul delighted "in weaknesses, in insults, in hardships, in persecutions, in difficulties" since through them he experienced strength (2 Corinthians 12:10).

When I first read of Paul boasting about and delighting in his weaknesses, I can honestly say I was confused. Who would want to brag about things they don't do well? As a people pleaser and perfectionist, the mere thought of boldly airing my dirty laundry to the public embarrassed me. I believed my influence was only good if it was polished to the appearance of perfection. As I began to understand and actually experience the power of the Holy Spirit more in my life, it made more sense why Paul would choose to delight in weaknesses.

Boasting about our weakness isn't about belittling ourselves. It's also not about pride in doing the wrong things. Boasting about our weakness is merely acknowledging we are incapable of living perfectly without the power of Christ. Pressure to perform is released. The expectation to meet a certain standard is null. We receive freedom in confessing our imperfections and do not have to attempt to be perfect to live out of love. From that love flows grace and mercy. God knows that even though He has gifted us the power of his Holy Spirit by the death and resurrection of Christ on the cross, we will still mess up. He knows that on this side of eternity, our flesh will remain at war with our spirit, and therefore, we will continue to struggle with operating out of fear and love. This is why grace and mercy still abound.

There's so much peace in knowing that God understands our human frailty yet still offers to help us through. I began to heal from my depression when I understood that I was empowered by the Holy Spirit yet still covered with mercy. By the grace of God, the cloud of pressure began to lift. I didn't feel like it was an all-or-nothing kind of healing. I continued to have bad days, but eventually, those bad days turned into bad moments that became far and few between. God could have taken it all away in the snap of a finger; I don't doubt that. The progression of my mind healing more and more over time, though, is what gave me confidence in my faith. I know that I am prone to depression. I know that my weakness is self-hate, but I also know that the Spirit that dwells inside me is stronger.

My prayer is that you, too, regardless of your weaknesses, would experience the freedom of living by the Spirit.

> "I am the vine; you are the branches. If you remain in me and I in you, you will bear much fruit; apart from me you can do nothing."
>
> —John 15:5

Chapter 2

Sprouting

I was raised in the church. My family made no exception on Sunday mornings- church was a priority. We prayed before dinner. We joined small groups as a family. We attended church picnics and church functions. I was put in Awanas and attended Christian summer camps and retreats. Church played a pivotal role in my upbringing as a child. I would consider myself fortunate to have Christian parents who desired to expose me to truth during my formative years. I am grateful to have been raised with church at the forefront.

The interesting thing about being raised in the church, though, is how easily we can fall into unmanageable expectations that twist the Word of God. I know this doesn't apply to everyone who was raised going to church. On the other hand, I know that many of us have experienced a great deal of pressure to appear a certain way. Whether self-imposed or by influence of our church, encouragement toward Godly obedience can quickly turn into allegiance to maintaining a false perception of perfection.

At times, we view Biblical standards as expectations we are

capable of and responsible for maintaining by our own will. It's all too easy to forget grace in the reality that we all fall short of God's standard, and that salvation is a gift from God (Romans 3:23-24 & Ephesians 2:8-9 ESV). I see so much value in regular church attendance, and at the same time, I want to be clear that church is not what saves us. Church is a place to build authentic community rather than a place we go to put on a fake smile and pretend as if we were the epitome of a "good Christian."

Have you ever walked into a church and felt painfully out of place? It felt like you were the black sheep amongst a crowd of spiritual people you could never match up to. Unfortunately, this is why many people shy away from church. They don't believe they are good enough to step foot in a place like that. Even if they hear "come as you are," they don't believe it. The church has to do better. *We* have to do better.

Don't get me wrong; there are genuinely amazing, God-fearing people who attend church. At the same time, there are a bunch of fakers who attend church and do a really good job of hiding their sins. I would know because I've been one of them. I bought the lie that church was the place to be perfect. I wanted others to see me as a "good Christian" to the point I had even convinced myself I was one. I didn't understand the concept of grace and had no idea of the importance of being authentic in my faith by being truthful about my shortcomings. I thought the best influence on other people was to fake my way through faith so they would see the positive side of Christianity. I memorized the verses and attended church services and functions, yet my relationship with God felt transactional. With each "correct Christian behavior," I made a new deposit in my Christian piggy bank. My inability to maintain this facade became too much to keep up with. Each sinful choice was accompanied by a withdrawal full of interest. Eventually, my overspending became evident, and *I was the one* who felt grossly out of place attending church.

My misconception of church came from my misunderstanding of God. I've heard on numerous occasions that when we misunderstand who God is, it's often due to negative views we have about our relationship with our parents or ourselves. Similar to father wounds, our overall understanding of God is often initially a reflection of how we view those relationships.

As a child, I knew my parents loved me, but I didn't love myself. My lack of love for myself made it nearly impossible to see correction as a means of protection. I only felt affirmed by my parents when I felt like I was being "good." I took discipline very hard. I interpreted it as a result of my failure to be good. I didn't understand the concept of consequences and merely saw myself as bad when I was being disciplined. Because of this, I only accepted love when I thought I deserved it or earned it. I believed my mistakes deemed me "bad" and unworthy of love unless I did something positive to earn it back.

As I continued to grow into pre-adolescence, my drive to be accepted became the most twisted version of perfectionism. My disgust for myself and my imperfections became all-consuming. I *needed* to be perfect, but I was excruciatingly aware of my imperfections. The internal chaos I faced daily became unbearable to the point where mirrors became my worst enemy. I couldn't stand to look myself in the eyes.

> *"Dreading torture, looking in the mirror,*
>   *Knowing I'll never meet perfection.*
>   *Every glance into the glass,*
>   *I am more disgusted."*

At 12 years old, I began to write poetry expressing how much I hated myself. The terrible words and names I had become used to labeling myself felt better written out. I would never even think to say the same things about someone else, but somehow, I felt justified in my self-loathing. The hateful poetry became an outlet (so I thought) to let go of the dark things I was constantly thinking about. I found it therapeutic. However, time would tell that I was adding gasoline to a fire that Satan had lit early on in my drive to be "good" and in my predisposition to be so self-critical.

I was introduced to self-harm by a peer in my 6th-grade class. Soon after hearing her talk about her experience, I saw a couple of clips of a documentary on Marilyn Manson's followers who carved words across their skin. Because it had become so routine for me to think, write, and say such hateful things about myself, physically hurting myself seemed like the next reasonable thing to try. I was a failure at bullying myself into perfection and needed to take a new approach.

Surely, physical punishment was what I needed...

The first time I harmed myself is still so vivid that if I close my eyes and think about the moment, I am taken back to that little girl sitting on her bedroom floor sobbing and calling out to God, "God, why are you letting me do this to myself?" I cried the words out loud as I began to mark up my skin.

I was confused as to why a so-called loving God would allow somebody to do such a dark thing. I believed if He truly loved me, He would never have allowed me to experience so much hate and pain in the first place. As I continued to cut my arm and as God did not put a stop to it, I was sure that the physical pain and markings were exactly what I deserved.

Similar to the outlet I felt in writing such awful things about myself, cutting became another outlet to release the appalling thoughts I held inside. The marks on my body became a symbol of who I was...unlovable, unworthy, imperfect, failure. I quickly became addicted to cutting. As my appetite for self-harm grew, the words in my journal became darker and my thoughts more morbid.

> "Dying inside has never been so strong
> Crying outside is how I get along
> I can't take this much longer
> My fatal thoughts getting stronger
> I won't live like this much longer."

Part of me was desperate to feel okay, while the other part of me wished death would come. I recall many nights I wished and prayed I wouldn't wake up. After intentionally taking too many pain pills one night and falling asleep to the room spinning, I was disappointed when all I felt the next morning was nausea. Again, the reality of being a failure hit me like a brick.

Soon after my addiction to self-harm was full-fledged, I discovered the art of restricting food and the euphoric feeling I felt when my stomach was empty. If I couldn't release the hate from my body through the drops of my own blood, perhaps not filling my stomach would relieve the pain. Despite my efforts to curb the hate I felt for myself by controlling my intake, my hate only became stronger.

> "I want to get the blade out
> Cut my breath to gasps
> But first I must waste away
> Relive and relieve my past."

I had become a glutton for self-punishment. The horrific cycle of self-abuse I was in was an out-of-body experience. It was demonic. Satan had a grasp on me that felt impossible to get out of.

I didn't realize it at the time, but in hindsight, I see that though Satan had a grasp on me, he did not have me. He influenced me but did not own me. My introduction to Christ at a young age led me to receive His salvation at five years old. Though I did not understand the depth of that decision at my young age, I had welcomed Jesus into my heart. I see now that Satan didn't have ultimate authority over me.

Set Apart - Imago Dei

> "So God created man in his own image, in the image of God he created him; male and female he created them."
>
> — Genesis 1:27 ESV

"Imago Dei," or "image of God," defines the very quintessence of our design. From the beginning, we were chosen to be image-bearers of Elohim, the "Almighty God." Nothing else in creation was made to reflect God in the way that we were. You and I were created with spiritual, intellectual, and moral intricacies that stand out above every other living creature. We are recognizably different from the great creatures of the land, sky, and sea. Our ability to imagine, feel, think, reason, and remember is distinct. We are, by nature, set apart. A simple Google search tells us to be set apart means to be kept separate and for a special purpose. Not only do we stand out above all other creatures but our purpose is special. We are so special, in fact, that God's response to creating us was different from His response to the rest of creation. When He made everything else on earth, He "saw that it was good"

(Genesis 1:9, 1:12, 1:18, 1:21, 1:25; NLT). However, when God made us, He saw "it was *very* good!" (Genesis 1:31 ESV). On day one through five of creation, God was pleased, but on day six... when He formed mankind, He was exceptionally pleased. He was *delighted*. Our formation on the sixth day was the icing on the cake. Our design sweetened the rest of creation so much that it signified the completion of creation. Did you catch that? Earth was not complete *until God made us*. He did not rest until man was formed. It was as if God was saving the best for last.

> Thus the heavens and the earth were completed in all their vast array. By the seventh day God had finished the work He had been doing; so on the seventh day He rested from all His work. Then God blessed the seventh day and made it holy, because on it He rested from all the work of creating that He had done.
>
> — Genesis 2:1-3

Significance & Purpose - Imago Dei

Not only are we clearly different from all other creatures but we were given dominion over the rest of God's creation (Genesis 1:26 ESV). If you've ever climbed to the top of a mountain and had a 360-degree view of the surrounding landscape, you have probably felt incredibly small. If you've stood underneath the shade of a redwood tree, overlooked the Grand Canyon, or sat beside a cascading waterfall, you may not have just felt small but perhaps insignificant as well. Now, think of all the magnificent animals in the wild - the enormity of a lion's paw, the width of a whale's mouth, the weight of an elephant. Imagine yourself surrounded by all of earth's delights and knowing, despite how small you feel, you were given rule over every one of them. This is quite the opposite of insignificance.

I don't know about you, but when I close my eyes and picture a mountain top, trees, canyons, waterfalls, and great creatures of this world, I am in complete awe. It's difficult to wrap my mind around the truth that we were created as greater than all these things *and* made to rule over the earth. Quite frankly, the significance of our being too often falls short on me.

The significance of being designed as Imago Dei doesn't stop at creation. The significance of our Imago Dei lies in our God-given purpose. God didn't create us out of arrogance or loneliness. *He created us out of love.* The Triune God: Father, Son, and Holy Spirit, is a God of relationship and our very purpose is to love Him and love others. That's why, when asked what the greatest commandment is, Jesus responded, "'Love the Lord your God with all your heart and with all your soul and with all your mind. This is the first and greatest commandment. And the second is like it: 'Love your neighbor as yourself. All the Law and the Prophets hang on these two commandments" (Matthew 22:36-40). It is written on our hearts to love and to be loved, and our greatest purpose is only fulfilled when we are living in the love of our Father.

To love God and know God is to build a relationship with Him. Building a relationship with God is similar in some ways to building a relationship with another person. There is a requirement for vulnerability, however, vulnerability is different with God. In a deep relationship with another person, we mutually are required to open our hearts in a way that is risky. We don't know how the other person will respond when we open ourselves up to them. They may accept us, or they may reject us, but that is the risk that is necessary to develop a meaningful relationship with another person. God *desires* but does not *need* for us to open up to Him in such a way. *He already knows us.* We aren't risking rejection because we are already accepted. Let me repeat that. *There is no risk of rejection in getting to know God because He already knows, accepts, and loves us.* Discovering this is an incredibly freeing experience.

If you can't see this yet for yourself, there are numerous accounts of God knowing and loving people before they knew Him throughout the Bible. Story after story shows people throughout the Old and New Testament experiencing the revelation that God knows and accepts us before we know Him.

God had a plan for Jeremiah before he was conceived.

> "I knew you before I formed you in your mother's womb. Before you were born I set you apart and appointed you as my prophet to the nations."
>
> — Jeremiah 1:5 NLT

God knew the course of King David's life before he was born.

> "You saw me before I was born. Every day of my life was recorded in your book. Every moment was laid out before a single day had passed;"
>
> — Psalm 139:16 NLT

God cared deeply about what Moses was doing and knew him intimately.

> "The Lord replied to Moses, "I will indeed do what you have asked, for I look favorably on you, and I know you by name;"

Tiffany Sullivan

— Exodus 33:17 NLT

God claimed Israel as His own.

"But now, this is what the Lord says—
 he who created you, Jacob,
 he who formed you, Israel:
 Do not fear, for I have redeemed you;
 I have summoned you by name; you are mine."

— Isaiah 43:1

What a relief it is to come into a relationship with someone who already knows and accepts your darkest secrets! I'll never forget the conversation I had with my husband (who was only a friend at the time) regarding my relationship with another woman. After a failed relationship with a Christian man who clearly had issues with the fact that I had dated a woman, I was scared to tell anyone else about that part of my life. As soon as I blurted out that I had dated another woman, (my now husband) responded by saying, "Who?" and then said her name. He was unfazed. I, however, was in shock he knew her previously and somehow had put two and two together the moment I word-vomited my secret. His nonchalant response took a load of pressure off of me. I didn't feel anxiety or a need to explain myself. The immediate acceptance of my past and of me was evident in his tone of voice.

The scariest part about developing a deep relationship with another person is exposing the raw parts of us. The risk of letting someone new into the darkest corners of our hearts and minds is all too terrifying. When you experience someone knowing and accepting you as is, there is a comfort in knowing it's okay to be who you are, messy past, messy present, and all.

It is astounding that God has always known our delicate and most horrifying parts and still loves us with an incomparable love. In His perfection, God has every right to reject us and leave us to our sinful natures, but instead, He invites us in.

If God already knows us, why then would we want to talk to Him about our dark secrets? Why would we want to relive our pasts or have to think about the things we are ashamed of? We do it to experience His healing. We do it to experience His grace. We do it to experience the sweetness of undeserved mercy. When we open our hearts to the Lord, we begin to change. We start to understand, know, and see Him more. As we understand, know, and see God more, our true identity becomes clearer.

We have a lot to learn when it comes to understanding just how wide and how deep the love of our Father goes. It takes time. Knowing God comes by reading His word, praying, sitting in His presence, and through relationships with other believers. As we grow in our relationship with God, we start to grasp the gravity of how great His love truly is, and in turn, we can understand our position as Imago Dei bearers in this world. "When people see themselves the way God sees them, as His wonderful works and particular reflections of His image, then they see what is inside of them and perceive the universe in a different way (Psalm 139:14). Each of us is meant to bear his glory in our unique way- we all have a beautiful way of stewarding eternity (Ecclesiastes 3:11; Genesis 1-2)."[1]

Not only were we created for love here and now, but we were created for eternity. God loves us so much that He desires to spend eternity with us. He sent his son, Jesus Christ, to be the catalyst that we may live with Him into eternity. Christ, the perfect Son of God, came to earth and died for our sins. We are the object of affection of the One Most High in the greatest love story of all time (John 15:13 NKJV).

> "For we are His workmanship, created in Christ Jesus for good works, which God prepared beforehand that we should walk in them."
>
> — Ephesians 2:10 NKJV

The Enemy Knows Our Weakness

The devil knows the purpose God has for each of us and despises it. He hates God. He hates good. He hates us. Satan stands to destroy every good and holy thing that God wants to do through us. He uses our humanity against us and does everything he can to get us to live by our flesh instead of the Spirit. He started with Adam and Eve in the garden knowing their flesh was weak. If he can influence us to act out of our weaknesses, he knows our spirit will become beaten down and that, eventually, we will question God's presence and goodness in our lives. His goal is to separate us from God eternally.

> "Out of a person's heart, come evil thoughts, sexual immorality, theft, murder, adultery, greed, wickedness, deceit, lustful desires, envy, slander, pride, and foolishness. All these vile things come from within; they are what defile you."
>
> — Mark 7:21-23 NLT

Even though we are image-bearers of God, we are born imperfect in our hearts (Jeremiah 17:9 ESV). Sometimes, our biological makeup causes us to be prone to certain hardships.

Mental illness can be a result of our experiences. It can also be a result of genetics and generational trauma. My struggle with depression was a result of both. My natural state is not happy-go-lucky. My natural state leans towards pessimism, and I am a glutton for self-punishment. My family history speaks to my inclinations as well. Generation after generation, my bloodline proved to predestine me to struggle with dark thoughts. Family history of mental illness? Check. Suicide, suicidal attempts, and ideations within the family? Check and check. Satan knew that the struggles from both sides of my family and my brain chemistry were the perfect storm. He used what was uncontrollable to me to his advantage. Just like my weaknesses, he knows the struggles you are inclined to.

> "Be alert and of sober mind. Your enemy the devil prowls around like a roaring lion looking for someone to devour."
>
> — 1 Peter 5:8

It is important to be conscious of our weaknesses because we are a target of Satan. Staying mindful of where we easily lose ground can make or break the difference in whether we struggle from time to time or spiral out of control. Struggle and temptation are inevitable (John 16:33). Just because we are prone to struggles and temptation does not mean we must give in to our weaknesses. The enemy would like us to believe otherwise. He wants us to believe that as soon as we are tempted, we have failed. He wants us to assume that when we feel weak, we are already sinning. When we do not stay mindful of Satan's tactics, we fall for his lies and find ourselves further from our God-given right of freedom from sin. *"If you were really a Christian, you wouldn't think that way." "You must not love God if you feel like that." "You looked once so what's the difference in looking again?"* His lies leech with shame and guilt to drain us of the hope we were given through Christ.

I believed his lies. I lived in shame and guilt before I ever made the decision to self-harm. With every lie I believed, I moved further and further away from God. The truth I heard all the years growing up in church became a distant recollection as I replaced truth with the lies that I was unlovable, unworthy, and imperfect. I allowed God's perfect love that casts out all fear (1 John 4:18) to be overtaken by hatred. As I struggled more and more with depressive thoughts, Satan continued whispering lies to me... *"If God were a loving God, He wouldn't allow you to hurt like this." "If God is truly all-powerful, he would stop you."*

I began to believe the lies and respond accordingly. In turn, I spiraled out of control into an all-consuming addiction to self-mutilation. The more I spiraled, the more beaten down I felt. The more beaten down I felt, the more convinced I was that I would never be free from self-hatred. The devil thought he was winning...

I want to be clear on one thing: although the devil influenced me, *my* choices were ultimately what drove me further from God. "The devil made me do it" is a cop-out people use to avoid responsibility. I can understand the desire to blame shift, but there is power in owning our choices. We are empowered to choose when we acknowledge we are responsible for our own decisions. And if you have received Christ as your Savior, you are covered by his Holy blood and empowered by the Holy Spirit. You have authority over any demonic strongholds you may experience. With that being said, the task of choosing differently is, more often than not, incredibly difficult. For many of us, it is not a simple decision to do better but a daily state of allowing God to work through us.

Addictions rewire the brain, and most people who repeatedly find themselves bound to their addiction require intensive therapeutic help. Choosing to get help is a great first step to combating addiction.

Do you find yourself easily reverting to certain detrimental thought patterns or behaviors? Is there a dark cloud of family history that has deeply impacted you and your choices? Do you feel beaten down because you can't seem to move past the cloud? Do you wonder if God forgot about you? Are you questioning if God even loves you?

I get it.

It's easy to question God when life becomes hard. Even if you've seen triumph in your life but find yourself struggling again, it's normal to wonder where God is. Any feeling of being beaten down, guilt, or shame, is not from God. He doesn't want us to live in darkness. He wants us to live in His love and in His light. He wants us to live with joy in His freedom. That is why He walks with us through hard seasons and why He wants us to seek Him in the midst of troubles. He is the one true and lasting source of comfort. As believers, He has given us the opportunity and authority to experience difficulties in a way no one else can. By the death and resurrection of his Son, the Holy Spirit came to give us a way out of the dark places.

Sprouts of the Spirit

I've heard many times in many different ways that God must not exist if there is so much suffering in the world. Some say people wouldn't be born with disabilities, mental illness, or deadly diseases if there was a God. Many people have fallen away from faith because they've gone through something hard and didn't see God in it.

I'm here to tell you that by suffering, we can see God more clearly.

My first few years as a Christian were easy. I simply believed in God because I had no reason not to. As I got older and found myself in turmoil, I began asking hard questions. *"God, why are you letting me do this to myself? Why would you let me feel this way if you actually loved me?"* The questions I had about God's realness and compassion were put to the test time and time again. All of those times have actually been lessons of His presence. Through all I have experienced in the rawness of life's challenges, my faith, which was weak, has become stronger. I once believed in a genie-like God who, at the snap of my fingers, should lift my burdens.

I now understand that my loving Heavenly Father allows us to go through hard times to experience His power more. If He merely snapped His fingers to move us out of a hard place, we wouldn't get to feel unexplainable peace in the midst of pain, unwavering grace that we don't deserve, and continuous mercies in the middle of mistakes. His greatness is revealed in our imperfect lives.

Growth is the result of hardship as well. I'm sure you've heard the saying, "One step forward, two steps back. Two steps forward, one step back." The path to growth is not a linear progression. The inevitable ups and downs in life are what make the journey beautiful. Without the lows, we wouldn't appreciate the highs as much. God is gentle and perfect in His timing as well. He allows us to go through difficult things and grow at a pace that is manageable (1 Corinthians 10:13 NLT).

Strong faith doesn't require a dramatic testimony, but I know from experience that even when God seems so far away, He is right there with us, waiting for us to release our burdens to Him.

Let's be clear: releasing our burdens does not mean

automatic relief. Releasing our burdens means we are handing them over to Christ who already carried them on the cross. It's letting go of our pasts and our presumed outcomes by trusting God to use *what was* to create *what will be*. Release is often not a one-off thing, either. Sometimes it's day-by-day, hour-by-hour, minute-by-minute, second-by-second. And every time we release something, we are paving the way for something greater. That "something greater" may be distinct in different seasons, but it's important to *recognize reality* and *remember*.

We recognize that this life isn't meant to be easy and acknowledge that we have an opportunity to have victory in every experience. We are warriors, and our battle belongs to the Lord. To have victory, we must remember. When we remember what God's word says about who He is and experience it firsthand, we become unstoppable. His word is an undefeatable weapon against our flesh and the devil. His Word ultimately leads us to victory in living exactly how we were created to be - wholly and Holy in Him.

> "The seed is the word of God. Those along the path are the ones who hear, and then the devil comes and takes away the word from their hearts, so that they may not believe and be saved. Those on the rocky ground are the ones who receive the word with joy when they hear it, but they have no root. They believe for a while, but in the time of testing they fall away. The seed that fell among thorns stands for those who hear, but as they go on their way they are choked by life's worries, riches and pleasures, and they do not mature. But the seed on good soil stands for those with a noble and good heart, who hear the word, retain it, and by persevering produce a crop."
>
> — Luke 8:11-15

Chapter 3

Dry Lands

I lost my purity ring at a "Girls of Grace" conference when I was a teenager. There's some irony there when I think about the period of my life later on when I dated another woman. Leading up to my relationship with her, I had experienced a new sense of purity. So, as we dated, I felt like I lost purity and had fallen from grace. As if foreshadowing, losing the ring felt like losing part of the identity I had always known.

For most of my life, my understanding of purity was what you would expect from a girl raised in a Christian church. I had fantastic youth pastors; however, I developed the same thought process on sex that has earned many eye rolls from non-Christians. Any interest in or curiosity about sex was taboo. In my mind, sex and all things surrounding sex *was* the forbidden fruit. Purity was the hottest topic to discuss with Christian youth entering puberty. It's now negatively referred to as "purity culture." There was a hyper-focus in youth groups, at youth rallies, and at conferences on dressing modestly and maintaining sexual purity. Parents were recommended specific books to give their teens to learn about sex and purity. I believe the general intent was well-meaning, but the messaging was more often than not poorly executed.

We were told modesty, a biblical standard, was dressing in a way to avoid tempting the opposite sex. Modesty never pertained to attitude but rather physical appearance and was always directed towards the girls. Because of this, I believed females were the ones who held power over males who seemingly couldn't control their thoughts or actions when we dressed a certain way. We girls were directed to "protect our brothers in Christ" by our choice of clothing. The implication was that purity came down to the responsibility of the female population.

We were also encouraged to make promises to stay "pure" (aka remain virgins) until marriage. Purity rings were the "it" thing in my Christian circle of friends. Purity rings became a badge of honor and a symbol of being a "good Christian." When I received my ring (which had a real diamond in it), I thought I was something special. I put that ring on every day with pride in knowing that my virginity was something to brag about. I wore that ring and knew as long as I wore it, I had value.

When I lost that ring, I was very upset. I felt like something was missing from me, and as if by not wearing it, I automatically was less modest and more of a temptation. I begged my parents to get another one. I needed something on my finger to show the world that I was better with it. My parents agreed to buy a new ring, but it had to be a less expensive one without a diamond. I was disappointed I wouldn't have a diamond any longer but was so excited to go to the Bible SuperStore (if you know, you know) to pick out my new ring. I decided on a silver ring that read "True Love Waits" across the band. I thought it was the perfect replacement. The purpose of the ring was much more obvious to the onlooker. Now, instead of wondering if my diamond ring was a promise ring from a boy, people would see the words and know how much willpower I had and how special I was. Whenever I was asked about it, I proudly explained I had decided to wait until marriage to have sex. I wore that ring for years and talked openly about my decision to wait for marriage. My openness about waiting even earned me the right to sit on a panel of teenagers and parents during a conference for younger teenagers. I sat in front of those younger Christians with pride as I shared my decision to remain pure. I was a good Christian and proud to be someone they could look up to (cue the eye rolls). Purity had become my god.

Religion is Barren

I have a soft spot in my heart for people who were raised in a Christian household and have decided to walk away from the faith. I know for many, it was a very difficult decision. With all of the current cultural issues, it seems there's been a rise of people who have decided to deconstruct *their* Christianity. I emphasize "their" because true Christianity is not something that can be deconstructed. Deconstruction, by definition, is to analyze analytically with the general purpose of exposing inaccuracies.[1] If the Word of God is infallible (which is what Christianity embraces as truth), then deconstruction is not possible.

Some people consider deconstruction to be questioning one's faith. Many people who have gone through a deconstruction describe it as if they are merely evaluating faith to reform it to what is true in their eyes. In reality, these people generally take out the parts they don't believe are socially moral. Topics like women's reproductive rights and same-sex marriage are frequently a point of contention from the perspective of the deconstructing Christian. It is a turning away from previously taught biblical standards they believe to be unfair or incorrect. Alisa Childers, a former Christian recording artist turned apologist, says, "Deconstruction isn't questioning your faith or wrestling with things you have been taught as a kid. It is the walking away from historic Christianity."[2] Meaning that those who decide to deconstruct aren't exposing inaccuracies in biblical teaching; they are rejecting biblical teaching.

I've often found myself thinking about why deconstruction seems to be trending lately. It would be easy to blame the church, and arguably, in some cases, rightfully so. Some would say the peak is due to the indoctrination of the stereotypical Christian family. I would argue that the people who find themselves deconstructing their faith have put too much weight on religion and likely have either never understood or have never experienced an authentic relationship with Christ. No judgment there. I can relate. Many of us who grew up in the church fell into some sort of pressure to be religious. Whether the pressure came from a specific person or church group or was self-imposed, there was an immense desire to become a "good Christian." The aspiration still exists in many Christian circles, as if an unsaid reward system is available to the people who succeed at following religious instructions. The endless striving to become more "Christian" inevitably becomes exhausting.

It makes sense that so many people would misunderstand the Christian faith. Obedience and independence are at odds within us beginning in childhood. We are inclined to respond to instructions while simultaneously desiring freedom of choice. Part of us thrives in structure and with boundaries; at the same time, we crave autonomy. I see this often with my toddler. When I give him a task, he is usually excited until the boundaries I give him do not align with his desire to complete it however he wants—feeding the dog, for example. He loves scooping the food into her dish and does not understand that we only give her one scoop at a time for a reason. Occasionally he continues to try and put more food into the dish. When I put a stop to it, he only sees that I am putting an end to what he was set on doing. He doesn't realize that giving the dog an excess of food is actually harmful and how my instruction is intended for protection.

Understanding and following God's Word can be similar. God gives us independence and autonomy to choose; however, He sets boundaries for us. He sees the harm we do not. He wants to protect us from the pain that will come when we veer away from His boundaries that were created for our good. It's hard to see it that way, though, until we've experienced the consequences of making choices that don't align with God's will. Unfortunately, we tend to learn best by experiencing the pain of poor choices, like touching a hot stove. We are told about the danger of touching it, but until we actually feel the burn of our skin on its hot surface, we don't fully grasp the danger.

Understanding godly standards has to come from the perspective of relationship. If it does not, true meaning and purpose are lost in translation. Without the relationship aspect, Christianity would be a lot like barren lands if you ask me. The soil would be void of the nutrients necessary to grow vegetation (the fruits of Christ working in us). It would merely be another religion lacking the beauty and growth that comes from a genuine relationship with our Creator. In religion, there is nothing to nurture; therefore, nothing will flourish. Instead, religion is about standards you either live up to or you don't. There isn't room for human error. It is empty of grace and mercy and leaves all the responsibility up to us. It also causes judgment to overrule our love for others.

I'll let you in on a little secret: if you have a religious mindset, you won't ever live up to godly standards—no one will. The standards are unachievable without a relationship with Christ. I'm telling you this because I've been there. I've been that person blinded by religion. Being religious made me believe that judgment of others was a sign of my righteousness when, in reality, it was a symptom of my self-righteousness. Being religious kept me hypocritically in denial of my humanity and held me back from experiencing the strength that comes with humility.

If I am tempted now to judge others for their decision to pick apart the Christian faith, God is so kind in reminding me of His patience. Before I experienced walking away from faith myself, I didn't realize how lost I would feel without God. I hadn't been faced with the dark reality of eternity without God until I was no longer walking with Him. He patiently allowed me to walk through such darkness so that I could eventually experience the greatest light possible on this side of heaven.

Perhaps you are experiencing this for yourself. I want you to know that I am here for you. I understand why you feel the need to take a step back to figure out what you believe. I recognize that what you want is truth, and I pray you encounter that.

Perhaps you are witnessing a dear friend or family member struggling in their faith. Don't lose hope. The best thing you can do is pray. And the next best thing you can do is listen and hear your loved one's heart.

> "Let any one of you who is without sin
> be the first to throw a stone at her."
>
> —John 8:7

Religion is the Gateway to Self-Righteousness

"You're pretty religious, aren't you?" I've heard this many times and can't say I particularly like the question. Though it is a good opportunity for further conversation, I wouldn't consider the label "religious" a compliment. Especially in recent years, being asked if I am religious has caused me to evaluate how I actually live out my faith in the presence of others. I wonder whether outsiders are seeing my genuine heart for God or a cleaned up version of myself that is fake.

Being fake in faith is quite easy to fall into when we focus on the do's and don'ts in the Bible. Even while developing a relationship with Christ, we can start to worship the Christian to-do list. Did you read the Bible today? Check "yes" if you're a good Christian. Did you go to church on Sunday? How about during the week? Did you tithe? Did you serve at church? How many small groups are you in? How many times did you pray today? The list, though full of good to-do's, is a distraction when our heart is not in the right place.

The slope is especially slippery for those who struggle with people-pleasing and perfectionism. We like lists of expectations because when we check something off, we tend to feel better about ourselves. Attending church becomes less about community and more about showing face. Reading our Bible is constantly at risk of becoming meaningless on the to-do list rather than an intimate meeting with our Father. When it comes to others' perspectives of our faith, we are tempted to care too deeply about how others view us rather than how authentic we are. Perception is everything. Affirmation we get from knowing we did something the "right" way usually strokes our ego more than it should. We tend to overthink and to try to control. Flaws are the enemy. Mistakes cause us anxiety. Comparison rules our hearts. Deep down, we know we are never actually perfect enough, so we become sick with self-criticism. We lack grace for ourselves.

People-pleasing and perfectionism come down to the outward appearance of righteousness rather than the state of the heart. We put ourselves and our religion on the throne that is meant for the One who is perfecting us. We put ourselves in the driver's seat when we are meant to be the passenger. When we are stuck in a state of perfectionism and people-pleasing, we are getting in the way of what God wants to do in us and through us. God wants us to be made righteous by Him because He is the only way to perfection. Any appearance of righteousness that does not come from Him is not pure.

The Bible warns us about the dangers of self-righteousness repeatedly:

Being self-righteous makes us fake our love for God.

In Romans, Paul talks about how the Israelites were falsely zealous of God. "For I bear them witness that they have a zeal for God, but not according to knowledge. For they, being ignorant of God's righteousness, and seeking to establish their own righteousness, have not submitted to the righteousness of God." (Romans 10:2-4 NKJV). When we attempt to be righteous on our own, we don't truly know the Lord, so our love for Him is not real. We cannot work our way to God and to an intimate loving relationship with Him.

Being self-righteous makes us hypocrites.

The Pharisees were known for being religious and self-righteous. Jesus, using the example of the Pharisees, warns the disciples of hypocrisy. "There is nothing concealed that will not be disclosed, or hidden that will not be made known. What you have said in the dark will be heard in the daylight, and what you have whispered in the ear in the inner rooms will be proclaimed from the roofs." (Luke 12:2-3). No amount of appearing to have it all together will save us from judgment day. We cannot hide behind a religious façade- God sees right through it and sees our hearts exactly as they are.

Being self-righteous makes us unclean.

Jesus was the antithesis of the Pharisees. He was harsh on their religious ways and creative in how he addressed it. Jesus shared a meal with a Pharisee and intentionally did not wash before eating. When the Pharisees noticed, Jesus responded by saying, "Now you Pharisees make the outside of the cup and dish clean, but your inward part is full of greed and wickedness." (Luke 11:39 NKJV). Jesus used this scenario to call out the uncleanliness and unholiness of the heart of the Pharisees. When we focus so much on appearing to be a good Christian, even by our good duties, we are obstructing the opportunity God grants us to change us from the inside out. Jesus desires to clean our hearts but cannot do so when we spend our time and energy on appearing a certain way.

Being self-righteous leads others away from God.

When confronted for insulting the Pharisees, Jesus points out that the "experts of the law" burden people with loads they cannot carry, and they refuse to help them. He says that they are actually responsible for leading people astray by their expertise (Luke 11:46). Jesus knew how detrimental the idol of religion was. People are not attracted to Christianity when all they see is a fake version where followers are focused on "acting Christian," and authenticity goes out the window. Sincere humility and meeting others where they are is necessary to lead people to Christ.

Purified

Although there is a good argument for how religion turns people away from God, it must be said that the laws in the Bible aren't without reason. Have you ever heard the saying, "Cleanliness is next to Godliness?" In the Old Testament, God gave instructions to His people regarding cleanliness. The laws were extensive and very specific. Their purpose was for protection and to allow God's people to draw near to Him in their purification. The laws defined sin and were condemning yet pointed people to Truth and the need for a Savior. They set the tone for what would come in the New Testament when the prophecies of a Savior would be fulfilled. Because mankind is imperfect, God, in His loving kindness, sent His son to fulfill an impossible law for us (Matthew 5:17). God has always had a plan for purification through the sacrifice of Jesus Christ.

Purification isn't just a plan. It's as necessary to our souls as water is to our bodies. Access to clean water is critical for our health. Without it, we are exposed to preventable illnesses. The Bible emphasizes how crucial it is to wash our hands and purify our hearts (James 4:8 NLT). There is no sugarcoating the reason we need to purify our hearts - it's because we are double-minded. David felt this in the weight of his sin when he said, "Create in me a clean heart, O God, and renew a steadfast spirit within me" (Psalm 51:10 NKJV). On the one hand, we say we have faith in God, and on the other hand, we doubt His goodness and act sinfully on our own behalf. We are fickle human beings in desperate need for a deep cleaning of our hearts to remain faithful to what God has set out to do. It's not that we aren't considered clean when we receive salvation. By Christ we are washed clean, but we are still in need of purification (Hebrews 9:14 NLT). When we accept Christ, we are agreeing that the way we were formerly living wasn't right, and we agree to a life of transformation through the power of the Holy Spirit (2 Corinthians 3:18). Holiness is our new life (1 Peter 1:15-16 ESV). Holiness is a part of Christian living that makes us unlike everyone else. In other words, *we are set apart*. True holiness is marked by obedience and only comes through the purification of our hearts.

Much like the reasons to purify water for our physical health's sake, going through our own process of purification reduces the contamination in our hearts. This is not accomplished by our own effort but by the leading of the Holy Spirit. The Holy Spirit exposes what the Father wants to change in us (John 16:8 ESV). Just as a loving father will point his children in the direction that is best for them, our heavenly Father wants to do the same for us. The intimate moments we spend with God in prayer and reading His Word are what teach us about His transformative plan for us. These moments help train us to live according to His plan.

There are many different methods to purify water but what matters most is the outcome. The method God uses to purify us may look different in different seasons or may look different for different people but know that He never gives any of us more than we can handle (1 Cor. 10:13 NLT). An immediate overhauling of our corrupt hearts would be too much for most of us. The Lord knows and understands this. He is gracious and His timing is good (2 Peter 3:9 ESV). Sometimes, it may feel like we've actually reached our boiling point and cannot go any further, but God is faithful to provide what we need in those moments when we turn to Him. Walking in line with God and releasing our burdens to Him makes the heat bearable.

God often works in a way that slowly cleanses our hearts in a similar manner to the filtering of water. The Holy Spirit, acting as the filter, prompts us to stop whatever isn't meant to pass through. It's that moment of pause we encounter right before we do what we were set out to do. We don't always adhere to the prompt, and oftentimes, unclean particles make their way through the filter. But God, in His patience and lovingkindness, continues His purification work.

It does require a willingness on our part to experience God moving in us. Without any openness to be moved towards holiness, we will remain unfiltered with dust and dirt settled at the bottom of our hearts. With softened hearts, the sediment is able to be cleared out. I don't believe it's a coincidence that blood, essential to life, is engaged in a filtering process as well. Like blood, filtered in the kidneys, weaving throughout our veins and arteries to keep our physical hearts pumping, the water of life is meant to freshly flow through us spiritually. Blood that's unable to flow freely through our veins indicates blockage. Blockages put us at risk for heart attacks that are potentially lethal. When we continue to block God's filtering system with resistance and disobedience our hearts become hardened to the working of God. Hardened hearts ultimately become a place where stagnant water sits, bacteria begins to grow, and lives are permeated with a smell that resembles rotten eggs.

Maybe you find yourself stagnant and wondering if God is

even real. You may even have hope that God is real but doubt that He wants you. Maybe you know God is real, but you are so angry with Him because it feels like He's turned His back on you. Maybe the idea of purification scares you. What is God going to make me give up? What is God going to want me to do that I don't want to? Will I be able to handle it? We tend to look at God's plan for our lives through our own lenses of how our lives will be impacted, often forgetting God's protection and provision that leads to health and wholeness.

If you feel your heart is hard or if you are worried about what God is going to ask of you, I want you to know that your questions, your doubts, and your feelings are ever so important to God. He wants to know about it. He can handle it all. He wants us to come to Him with all our imperfections and our fears. He wants honest thoughts and feelings to be laid out in front of Him. Nothing we think or feel scares God. He created us to have thoughts and feelings and wants to be that safe place we choose to go to when times get too hard, when feelings get too strong, or questions get too big. Nothing is too much for Him to carry.

> "Don't ever hesitate to take to God whatever is on your heart. He already knows it anyway, but He doesn't want you to bear its pain or celebrate its joy alone."[3]

Questioning Faith

"Faith was never meant to be static or unchanging. Questioning your faith means you are taking seriously the task of pursuing truth and figuring out what it means to live according to it."[4]

Questioning my faith was not something I was taught to do and often felt like something I shouldn't do. I had the idea that questions would take me away from God instead of leading me closer to Him. Despite my former opinion on questioning, through hardships, I have found myself on multiple occasions asking God where He was or what He was doing. I've doubted God's goodness, questioned the truth of the Bible, and even wondered if I actually deserved a Savior, assuming hell was an appropriate place for me to end up. When I look back on those seasons of questioning, I am grateful I took the time to hash things out, so to speak. I am glad for the dark seasons in the wilderness because, ultimately, God always proved faithful, just, and good. The times I felt furthest from God ended up being the catalyst to draw me closer to Him than I had been before. Without the questions and without the hard times, I don't think I would have really understood just how much God loves me. In fact, I am still learning how deep His love really is!

I want to encourage you to welcome questions. Challenge your faith by asking God to show you where He is when He seems so far away. Ask God what He is doing when life seems so unfair or chaotic. Tell God how angry you are with Him. Be honest about your doubts. Let God bear the weight of your questions. And you know that cheesy Christian saying, "Let go and let God?" There's an annoyingly good point to the saying. It's not just for the chronic worries. It's also not a simple problem-solving answer. And it's definitely not reserved for the people who have more faith. Letting go is unleashing whatever emotions you are feeling. It's the release of what's prim and proper in Christianity and allowing the ugly thoughts and feelings out.

Our time with God doesn't have to look like us kneeling nicely at the end of our bed with our palms gently pressed together as we sweetly start our prayer, "Dear God..." No, our prayers can come by way of a tear-soaked face, fist-shaking, and shouting out, "God, what are you doing? Why are you allowing this pain?" Remember, true intimacy is created through authenticity.

I can recall many private moments with God where I was drenched in sweat, boxing gloves on, in an all-out war with punching bags. In my sweat-stained tears, anger saturated my questions about where He had me.

I didn't ask for this... Why, God, WHY?

While letting all hell loose on those bags, I felt permission to process my feelings as unkempt and ugly as they were. I felt free to be in the moment, raw and unabashed. Ultimately, *I felt accepted as is* while the hate, terror, and hopelessness that were weighing me down were worked out of me. The pain of how I was feeling needed an honest release because I was so hurt and completely confused. In these moments, the unhealed wounds of my situation weren't gone immediately, but letting loose the intense emotions I was harboring lifted tension and opened my lungs to breathe in fresh air.

After releasing such intense emotions, there's a stillness in the air. It's the calm *after* the storm. The leftover evidence of the storm remains, but the intensity is gone. The whipping of the trees and the whirling of the wind has ceased. Branches may be down, shingles may be missing, but the storm has passed. There's a peacefulness that rests in the aftermath... Cleanup still has to happen, but there's no need to hold your breath any longer, bracing for the impact. So it's not just "letting go" per se. It's letting loose. It's loosening the grip on what's about to destroy. It's taking time to take in what you've experienced. It's taking time to breathe. It's allowing yourself to see the mess that's left behind. And it's giving space to feel all of the human feelings as they are. Then, in the rawness of it all, it's allowing God to handle the "why?" It's allowing your soul to settle at the faint whisper, "It wasn't for nothing."

I want to point out the difference between asking God

questions and assuming He is the cause of our hurt. Especially when the pain we've experienced has been at the hands of other Christians. It's all too common to talk about church hurt in a way that blames God for sin and, in turn, excuses questioning God's truth and authority. I get why it happens. In theory, Christians should be the best examples of Christ. We want to believe that all Christians are living in accordance with what they say they believe. Churches should be a place we go to feel safe, and I know for many people, church was where they felt the most unsafe. The reality of the fallen man is a hard fact to come to terms with when we've been on the receiving end of such hurtful things. I've been on both sides.

When I was coming back to faith after years in the literal and symbolic wilderness, I was terrified and excited to make friends at a new church. I quickly connected with a few people within the young adult ministry and was friendly with everyone else. When I began dating my boyfriend (who is now my husband), I was also pursuing my newfound interest in bodybuilding. You know, those overly tanned, excessively lean, skimpily-clad people who flex on stage? Yeah, that was what I was aiming to achieve at that point in life.

I started to prepare for a show and was posting my physique progress and posing practice on Instagram. My intention was to share the inward healing I experienced in terms of my previous eating disorder, along with my progress in training for the show. I didn't think deeply into how the pictures or video clips appeared but apparently others around me did. I caught wind that some of the girls in leadership positions within the ministry I was attending had referred to my boyfriend and me as "the firefighter and the slut."

Thank goodness for the few people I had connected with closely and who knew where I was spiritually. I was in a tender place where I wanted to live for God but still had a lot of insecurities. My friends sat with me and listened to my heart without judgment. They heard my pain, helped me work through my feelings about the situation, and supported me in my decision to confront the girls for the hurtful things they had said.

In my discussion with those girls, I saw their humanity too. I no longer saw them on the leadership pedestal I had previously placed them on. I recognized that just because they were involved more in the ministry than I, it did not mean they were immune to sin. The entire situation, though hurtful, allowed me to receive grace and to give grace to other believers in a way I hadn't before. In a way, I felt less pressure to be perfect and more freedom to continue to allow God to do work within me.

As believers, it's so important to separate other Christians, who are all faulty, from the Perfecter of our faith. When we question God, we have to be careful not to give people so much power. Jeremiah 17:9-10, a commonly heard verse, reads, "The heart is deceitful above all things and beyond cure. Who can understand it? I the Lord search the heart and examine the mind, to reward each person according to their conduct, according to what their deeds deserve." When we don't take into account the brokenness of mankind and the need for a Savior for *all* people, even inside the church, we are prone to bear a greater weight when someone hurts us. In verse 5, the Lord actually curses the person "who trusts in man" and "draws strength from his flesh." He calls out this person as someone whose heart is turned away from Him. On the opposite side of the spectrum, in verse 8, He says the person who trusts Him and whose confidence is in Him is blessed. "They will be like a tree planted by the water that sends out its roots by the stream. It does not fear when heat comes; its leaves are always green."

You see when we base our question of God's goodness on

Coming Out Restored

the thoughts or opinions of imperfect believers, we are at risk of running dry. Eventually, without the watering of God's truth, our faith is bound to die. Don't let the world cloud your view of what God wants to do through your doubts. Let God search your heart and mind, then give space for Him to respond.

> "Search me, O God, and know my heart; Try me, and know my anxieties; And see if there is any wicked way in me, And lead me in the way everlasting."
>
> — Psalm 139:23-24 NKJV

Chapter 4

Fenceless Gardens

The story of my "True Love Waits" ring continues. The saga became even more twisted as I entered college and, for the first time, really faced sexual temptation. My sex drive was not raging, but my desire to be desired was...

I knew I had something so intriguing to the male species, and in my need to be validated and wanted, it became more and more difficult to hang on to what I thought made me so special—my virginity. As I received more attention from guys, I began to loosen the boundaries that church had strictly taught me to hold. Little by little, my innocence began to wane. Eventually, I found myself not saying no when I knew I should have. I moved my boundary line one too many times.

I felt used. I felt anything but special.

I was still technically a virgin, but a line was crossed where I felt like a fraud wearing my purity ring. I began to see myself as impure and dirty. The guilt I carried because of my choices was heavy. I blamed myself more than anyone else because I knew that even though I had been upfront about my boundaries, my body language and repeated pursuit of physical attention were telling a different story. Though I believe I was taken advantage of in some ways, I can't pretend I wasn't responsible for the parts I had control over. I continued returning to the people who did not respect my boundaries because I wanted to feel wanted.

A while later, I told my mom what had happened and said I didn't feel worthy of wearing my ring anymore. She did her best to reassure me. She knew how important my "purity" had been to me. Her reassurance felt like permission to still wear my badge of honor, however the shame I felt left me feeling impure and dirty.

I decided I would wear the ring upside down because I believed I deserved a reminder of what I had done and what I had lost. I thought it would be motivation to steer me back in the right, pure, and holy direction.

In the years that followed, the opposite happened. I became more promiscuous and eventually stopped wearing the ring altogether. My bare ring finger became a symbol of being a "bad Christian." I was no longer a good role model. I didn't just lose my virginity but lost what I thought my identity was as a Christian. The shame of not being able to maintain the sacredness of what I considered to be the best part of me - my sexuality - was unlike the shame I had experienced before.

I was 24 years old when I spiraled into another deep depression. I began to hate myself once again. I started to drink several nights a week. I was happier with myself and felt more confident the more I drank. I began using various forms of marijuana, sometimes in conjunction with drinking, to completely escape the truth of who I no longer was. I believed I was more enjoyable to be around when I was under the influence of alcohol and weed.

I hated myself, so I tried even harder to fill the void I felt with my shallow idea of love and acceptance. I wanted everyone around me to validate that I was a nice and fun person because, obviously, the Christian version of me was a failure.

Months went by of me engaging in destructive behavior after destructive behavior. Every day, whether I had alcohol the night before or not, I felt hungover. I never felt rested and always had a thirst I couldn't quench. I wanted more and needed more, but nothing would suffice. After months of trying to fill the void with alcohol, weed, and chasing guys, I realized I felt nothing anymore. I was numb. I wanted so desperately to feel something, so I reverted to cutting myself again. When the self-harm became a repeated pattern once more, I had a reality check. I knew I was in danger of completely losing control. I could feel myself disappearing into something so evil. The darkness that loomed over me began to scare me. I started to see that my attempts to control everything were actually causing me to lose control in a way I was all too familiar with.

At 24, I had mentally reverted back to 13 years old. The shame, the guilt, and the instability began to consume my every thought. By the grace of God, I truly wanted help and knew I could not battle this alone. I had been to counseling many times before, but this time, it was finally on my own accord. For my 25th birthday, I gifted myself the best gift ever - Christian counseling.

Boundaries and Identity

For far too long, I have relied on my role in relationships with other people to keep me feeling whole. Habitually, my worth has come from an unhealthy need to be wanted and needed. I have strived for too many years to be who others wanted me to be just to feel their love and acceptance. My acceptance of myself has come from the way I believe others see me. The effort I have put into controlling the uncontrollable is pitiful and the ways I have placed my value in the opinion of others are a complete waste of time and effort. I have codependency tendencies that have stolen many opportunities to grow because of my fear of what others may think. I have cheated others out of seeing the real, authentic version of me. I'm still in the process of recovering from my codependent tendencies. From what I have experienced so far, I can tell the process is not quick. Somedays it feels like I've just started and others feel like real progress has been made. Just as healing from anything else, healing from the need to be needed by other people takes time...

Those of us who have a tendency to be codependent depend on relationships in a very unhealthy way. With low self-esteem it seems nearly impossible to set and maintain a proper boundary. Our view of ourselves is often so intertwined with those in our lives that untangling the dysfunction means losing who we thought we were. We feel pain in our codependent relationships but even greater pain at the thought of being without the relationships. The fear of rejection and abandonment takes over any reason when we've been treated poorly. We have trained ourselves and those around us to function in dysfunction. The lack of health in our relationships is a driving force of our self-worth. When the other person is mad, we automatically believe it is our fault. Instead of setting limits, we set aside our own needs and go beyond our capabilities to try and fix what we think the other person needs. We tend to think we know best and act as if we are the main person responsible for helping others. As Christians, we don't like to admit it and often hide it with spirituality, but we have a savior complex.

Codependency is a lost identity through the desire to be essential to other people.

Hearing a verse like Proverbs 3:27 can be taken to the extreme. We read, "Do not withhold good from those to whom it's due, when it is in your power to act" (NKJV). We hear, "I know what's good for them. It's my responsibility to help." Us Christians who struggle with codependency tend to do less praying for the person and more doing for the person. We may say we trust God but we are constantly trying to help fix the problem that only God can fix. We ignore the fact that God works at different paces with different people and have made it our responsibility on our timeline to heal the people we love. Instead of listening, we talk about our opinion of how the other person should handle their life. We offer scripture, share podcasts, and send sermons we think the other person needs to hear. Though our efforts may appear righteous and godly, our "help" actually interferes. It interferes with our understanding of our own identity as well as others. Essentially, we are playing God, or rather making ourselves a god, idolizing our need to be needed by those around us.

The good news is there is help for us. We are offered healing by way of restored identity in Christ. Besides prayer and reading the Word, it takes work to get to a place of healing. It takes patience through trial and error to retrain the way we do relationships and to ultimately become healthier for ourselves and others. The process takes time to learn. It's often a completely new way of living in relationships.

The first place to start practicing is by building healthy boundaries within relationships. Everyone's boundaries will look different in the details, but the purpose will be similar - safety in the relationship. Simply put, a healthy boundary is an appropriate and helpful plan of action when another person is behaving in a way that may lead to an imbalance in the relationship, feelings of resentment, or exhaustion. You know it's a healthy boundary when your intent is not to control but rather to communicate your wants and needs while respecting and keeping others safe at the same time.

When we create healthy boundaries and stick to them, we can stand confidently in who we are without getting tangled in the web of codependency. We no longer base our feelings of self-worth on our relationships with others. We don't require certain responses from those around us to be okay with ourselves. We know when to put ourselves first and when to put others first. We find value in being separate from loved ones while maintaining appropriate support when support is needed. We also learn the difference between helpful and harmful support and no longer attempt to fix people. We are safe people. Instead, we allow others to grow through life at their own pace. We allow them to make mistakes because, quite frankly, we have no control otherwise. We are okay with the lack of control of others and are focused on what we can control for ourselves. We constantly reevaluate where boundaries are needed in relationships and desire to maintain healthy relationships. Broken boundaries become a place of personal responsibility. Broken boundaries become an opportunity for change rather than a way of life. And for once, with healthy boundaries, we finally start living more wholly in who we were created to be.

Broken Boundaries

Let me be blunt: no one else can break our boundaries.

Let me repeat that: no one else can break our boundaries.

They can, however, break our trust by disregarding or violating our boundaries, but they cannot *break* the boundaries. Only we can...This is something I have had to come to terms with. My desire to control too often gets in the way. I so badly want to set a boundary in a way that manages the other person's choices (hello, control issues). I'd like to tell people what I am and am not okay with in order to direct how they choose to interact with me. If only I could say, "You cannot speak to me like that," and they would give me the respect to never speak ill to me again, life would be so much easier.

The tough reality is that no matter how much I try, the only person I can blame for repeated broken boundaries is myself. It's a reality that those of us who struggle with setting boundaries have to face. It's often much easier to blame someone else for all our pain or discomfort. It feels better to hand the responsibility for the hard things we've encountered to someone else. A victim mentality is easier than facing any personal responsibility for how others have wronged us. Why should we be responsible for someone else's lack of respect for us?

Before we go further, I want to validate that some of you are truly victims of very traumatic and painful experiences that were absolutely out of your control. I am so very sorry that you were hurt in such an awful way.

I am not speaking about those circumstances. I am speaking to those of us who have let people walk all over us or have welcomed people into our lives in a way they do not deserve. I am speaking to those of us who have not done our part in having and maintaining healthy and safe relationships.

Hello, fellow poor boundary keeper. I am sorry we can relate in such a way. I wish we knew how to handle every relationship in our lives with confidence and ease. Not-so-ironically, the fixer in me would love to fix this for you. We are not broken, but there is a brokenness that has caused us to respond to people in such a way. It is important we learn how to have healthier relationships, but before we discuss that, we should talk about how we got to the predicament we are in.

Before the broken boundaries happened, there was a

fracture in our lives in how we received and understood love. From our first breath, we are completely dependent on others to survive; the need for love is imprinted on our very being. Over the next several years, as we learn to become more independent, our wiring for love remains constant. We know in our hearts that we were created for love and begin to see how we can get that need met by our behaviors. We likely don't understand the concept of identity, but we begin forming an understanding of who we are based on our interactions with those around us. We learn a reward and consequence system of what behaviors equal what responses from our parents, friends, teachers, siblings, etc. We are often taught about respect in how we treat others; "Treat others how you would like to be treated." The assumption is that kindness and care for everyone look the same. Make friends with everyone, share, and say nice things. These were the lessons I remember at least. These are fantastic lessons; however, I believe there are some important lessons that are missed at such an influential age.

 I don't recall a single lesson in school about standing up for yourself, *teaching* others how you would like to be treated, or fostering healthy friendships. Instead, we were left to learn about boundaries through rules given by adults, which many of us didn't understand the reason why. We heard, "Because I'm in charge," or, "Because this is how we do things." "Wouldn't you want so-and-so to do the same for you?"

 I realize age and brain development play a big part in how and when certain concepts are taught, but my point is that I believe poor boundaries are developed early for most of us because we want people to accept us. We want the adults in our lives to see that we are doing a good job, and we want the other children in our lives to be our friends. Our very nature is built on love and for love, so when we are merely taught about the giving side of relationships, we are more likely to develop a skewed idea of the receiving part of relationships.

As we continue to grow up, we learn more about life, and begin to hear about the idea of self-respect. Due to what we previously learned in relationships, some of us discover a false sense of self-respect. We equate self-respect with earning respect from our peers and begin to give too much trust to them. We give in to peer pressure. We don't want to appear weak or be called a loser. We view other people as "cool" and think what they must be doing is working, so why not try it? Eventually, we are in so deep with our attempts to be accepted that we excuse our decisions as acts of finding ourselves. This may mean meeting different types of people and trying new things to see where we feel we fit in best. Oftentimes we continue to try to gain love and acceptance from others by being someone we aren't actually comfortable with.

As we enter into adulthood, the poor patterns we were used to in relationships manifest by giving too much of ourselves to people who haven't earned the right. Our lack of self-respect and lack of knowing and accepting the real us causes us to allow people to be irresponsible with our hearts. We trade in authenticity for a false sense of security of the happiness or comfort of others over our own. We hand over our personal responsibility to other people and, in turn, sacrifice the peace and solitude of our hearts.

And here we are in a rut of giving permission to others to treat us how they would like. We so desperately want the love and acceptance of others that we are willing to bend and break our own boundaries in hopes we will be respected the next time. Without evidence of a change in behavior, we hear a promise of future respect and believe it because we see the good in the person.

Eventually, we get stuck in a dance of knowing how we

want to be treated and hoping that the other person will finally treat us with the love we have always wanted. They do the wrong thing, and we confront the issue. They say the right things, we cling to the hope of change, we continue to give them access to us, and eventually, we are back to them saying the right thing because they did the wrong thing again. The more we dance this dance, the less we believe in ourselves. The shame sinks in and the hope begins to fade, but we still cling to the tiniest glimmer of possibility that this time they will change. We want to be special enough for the other person to change. We will know we are valued and loved when they finally do something different. At the end of the day, though, we know deep down that they have acquired too much of us despite repeatedly proving they don't deserve it.

So, when we have broken boundaries, like Lysa Terkeurst discusses in her book "Goodbyes and Good Boundaries," we must face the reality that we have given away too much access to us. We are responsible for the access we give others. "Setting a boundary is being responsible enough to reduce the access we grant to others based on their ability to be responsible with that access. People who are irresponsible with our hearts should not be granted great access to our hearts. And the same is true for all other kinds of access as well- physical, emotional, spiritual, and financial."[1]

Poor boundaries are the root of many avoidable problems and stress we deal with. Without proper boundaries and the practice of holding to them, we are often left confused and heartbroken. One of the best visual illustrations I've heard to describe healthy boundaries is that boundaries are like property lines. They tell us where we begin and end and identify where we allow others to begin and end.

It's like planting a garden without working to create a proper bed for it to grow in. There is no line to define where the garden stops or ends, so the chances of weeds taking over are much more likely. To develop a thriving garden, you must first decide what you want to plant. Next, you pick where you want to plant the garden. You clear the ground, check the soil, and prepare the plant beds. *Then* you plant your plants. Once you have your plants in place, you must water regularly and protect and maintain the garden; otherwise, you are opening the door for dead plants and a garden overgrown with weeds.

When it comes to boundaries, typically, we know what we *want* a relationship to look like (i.e., we know what we want to plant), but when it comes to creating the defining line within our relationships, *our boundaries become tangled up between what we want and what we allow.* If we don't put in the time and effort to gauge what is appropriate and healthy in each relationship, we will likely water something we don't want growing in that garden.

How do we know if our relationship gardens could use some tending to? Here are a few signs:

- Having a hard time saying no. Whether to your boss, your significant other, your family member, your friend, or a stranger on the street, "No" may as well be a four-letter word.
- Others describe you as very sensitive and maybe even overly sensitive.
- Being uncomfortable in certain social settings and instead of speaking up or removing yourself, you sit in the discomfort.
- Justifying or making excuses for other people's behaviors that have a negative impact on you.
- Constantly feeling overbooked and overstressed.
- Laughing at things you don't actually find funny and actually find offensive or wrong.

- Trying to keep the peace when resolution is actually needed.
- Blaming yourself for the reaction of others.
- Making a decision is an incredibly hard task.
- Oversharing to anyone and everyone is a common occurrence.

If you resonate with any of these, chances are you can improve how you set and hold to your boundaries. You are not alone. For the record, I chose ten examples that I am still working on improving by implementing healthy boundaries. It will probably be a lifelong process of undoing all the negative habits I've created and I will likely be forever reevaluating and resetting what I allow in my relationships. I surely could be the keynote speaker at a seminar on how to struggle with setting boundaries and I would be a fantastic case study on what happens when you don't set or stick to your boundaries. I am constantly learning to own what is mine and let go of what is not.

Personal responsibility is the key to owning our role in boundary setting. We must acknowledge and accept what is in our control and stay on our side of the road. We have to understand that if we swerve onto the other side of the road, we are at serious risk of hurting ourselves and others. When we get into the habit of driving on our side of the street, any detours or distractions will be easier to get around. When it comes to being around repeated boundary violators, we need to step back and evaluate where *we* are repeatedly handing control to the violator. I understand how tricky it becomes when we live with or have family ties with someone who does not respect our boundaries, but until we take a solid stance on what is in our control, we will be powerless to codependence. Healthy boundaries help us stick to our responsibilities in the relationship and focus on our decisions within the relationship.²

Biblical Boundaries

The best place to learn about healthy boundaries is the Bible. Biblical boundaries were a foreign concept to me up until recently. I was under the impression that the Christian thing to do was always be nice no matter what. Do not ruffle any feathers and be a peacekeeper, even if it means sacrificing internal peace. We are told to turn the other cheek and show grace upon grace, right?

I mistook grace for giving up my well-being. Even if that meant apologizing for something I didn't do. Even if that meant offering to buy someone some necessities and when they took advantage of my generosity, not saying anything and instead allowing them to continue to rack up the bill. Even if that meant keeping someone close, though they continuously treated me poorly. I was very sick with codependency. Always the giver. Always the supporter. And always the enabler. I was a walking doormat. My poor boundaries caused me a lot of anxiety over the years and wreaked havoc on my self-esteem. Eventually I became closed off to new friendships and held other relationships at a distance. I've been a mess at healthy relationships but by the grace of God, in His restorative ways, I am learning what He says about boundaries.

The Bible shows us that boundaries *prepare us for eternity*. Eternity was placed in our souls at the beginning of time, and without God's boundaries, our eternity is at risk. Originating in the Garden, we see that God gave very specific boundaries regarding which tree to not eat from. When Adam and Eve ate from the tree they were told not to, they faced the consequence of their decision. They were sent away from the garden and were prevented from returning. Without the consequence, the risk that Adam and Eve would continue to eat from the tree and perpetuate their dying and sinful nature was high. That decision to keep eating from the tree would have had the greatest consequence of all; losing eternity with God. This was not something God was willing to make room for so He did not allow Adam and Eve to continue accessing the garden.[3] God does this with you and I as we grow to know Him more. He reveals boundaries to us in a way that prepares us for perfect eternity with Him. Heaven is an eternal reward that is a result of God's boundaries. It's where only purity and perfection can exist.

The Bible teaches us that boundaries are about *personal responsibility*. We must own what is ours. In Galatians 6:5, Paul says, "For each will have to bear his own load" (ESV). Every person comes with their own obligations and commitments in life. The authority we were given in this world did not stop at creation; we are called to work unyielding on our assignments. The Bible warns about idleness and says, "The one who is unwilling to work shall not eat" (2 Thessalonians 3:10).

In 2 Peter, we are reminded of our calling to live a godly life through God's "divine power" because we have "escaped the corruption of the world caused by evil desires." Peter talks about adding to our faith: goodness, knowledge, self-control, perseverance, godliness, mutual affection, and love (2 Peter 4-7). When we focus on what is ours, we have less time to worry about what is not ours, hence the instruction, "Seldom set foot in your neighbor's house— too much of you, and they will hate you" (Proverbs 25:17 NLT).

The Bible tells us boundaries have the *purpose of protection*. Jesus says during the Sermon on the Mount, "Do not give dogs what is sacred; do not throw your pearls to pigs. If you do, they may trample them under their feet" (Matthew 7:6). Jesus is likely speaking about repeatedly sharing the Gospel with people who continue to disregard and mock it. He often encountered disdainful religious leaders and was aware they were not receptive to hearing what He had to say. We must protect ourselves from people who have proven to lack respect for our boundaries. We must stop wasting our breath, hoping the other person will finally hear us. We must protect what is ours to protect.

We are called to be like Jesus. He is the prime example of compassion and the greatest sacrifice of love, and yet He had boundaries. He withdrew from crowds so He could go and pray (Luke 5:16 NKJV). When He told the disciples He was going to Jerusalem and would be crucified, Peter "took him aside and began to rebuke him." Jesus responded to Peter, saying, "Get behind me Satan. You are a stumbling block to me; you do not have in mind the concerns of God, but merely human concerns." (Matthew 16:21-23). Jesus turned from Peter's influence and stuck to what He knew must happen to fulfill God's will. Jesus knew His ultimate purpose was to live out God's plans for His life and wouldn't let anything or anyone get in the way of that. "For am I now seeking the favor of men, or of God? Or am I striving to please men? If I were still pleasing men, I should not be a servant of Christ" (Galatians 1:10 ASV). Boundaries are meant to point us toward Jesus and make us more like Him.

God is ever so intentional in providing boundaries. His love is exceedingly abundant in the way He gives limits. Our worship of God and the way we love ourselves and others is evident by the way we set limits ourselves. Boundaries don't come naturally to many of us so here are some ways we can learn about and practice Biblical boundaries:

Pray and be still to hear God. Spend time with God, praying about relationships where boundaries may be needed. Be silent with God so He can begin to direct your next steps (Philippians 4:6-7 ESV).

Gain Biblical insight. Spend time in God's Word to fight confusion by gaining wisdom on what kind of boundaries may be needed. The Word is our weapon (Hebrews 4:12 ESV).

Practice discernment. The extent of boundaries may look different for different people. Evaluate the relationships in your life that are with safe people and those that are not (1 Kings 3:9).

Use integrity. Be honest and upfront with behavior you will not accept and communicate ahead of time how you will respond (Matthew 5:37).

Own your true identity. Remind yourself of being made Imago Dei and the goodness that comes with that (Ephesians 2:10).

Be courageous. Be fortified by the power of God. He is trustworthy. He is for you and He will be with you in this process (Joshua 1:9 ESV).

Follow through. Hold true to your word by holding true to your boundaries so you may be trustworthy (Proverbs 12:22).

Give thanks. Let your boundaries be an act of worship. Praise God for His good and perfect love (Psalms 100:4-5 NKJV).

Pray for your enemies. When your boundaries are disrespected, pray for those who have hurt you (Matthew 5:44 NKJV).

Maintain a perspective of perseverance. Day after day, do the work that's yours. Release your relationships to the Lord and keep your eyes fixed on Jesus (Hebrews 12:1-2).

There is hope for change if you are a habitual poor boundary setter and keeper like me. When we do things differently in our relationships with pure motives of health and wholeness, we reap the rewards just as our relationships will reap the rewards. The process takes time, and we will experience trial and error, but the outcome is good with good intentions.

> "Whatever you do, work heartily, as for the Lord and not for men, knowing that from the Lord you will receive the inheritance as your reward. You are serving the Lord Christ."
>
> — Colossians 3:23-24 ESV

Chapter 5

Uprooted

My 25th birthday gift to myself, much-needed therapy, was a symbol of turning over a new leaf. I recognized I was getting sucked back into a deadly cycle and was desperate for a new life. I had been to counseling previously, but not truly on my own accord. My previous efforts to grow and heal were subpar at best. I describe those half efforts as "wanting to want it." I knew change was needed but, quite honestly, hadn't been willing to fully sacrifice everything I had to to see lasting change. I hadn't been ready to do the hard work yet. I had wanted the outcome without the effort I knew would be required of me to get there. This time, at 25, I felt rock bottom in a terrifying way and realized the only way out was to try something I hadn't tried before. I didn't want typical therapy. I didn't want to sit on a couch and talk about my problems. I wanted answers. I wanted resolution. I was finally ready to face the pain.

The counselor I ended up with was certified in a Christian faith-based approach to healing from emotional trauma. The goal of each session is to break through any emotions, thoughts, and beliefs the person is bound to. I was bound to depression, self-hate, and the belief that I deserved pain. The shame I felt for the parts of my life I wasn't proud of clouded all of the parts of me I should have been exceedingly proud of. Shame had taken over my identity, and I wanted to get to the bottom of it.

In my sessions with the counselor, two very significant details that spurred my destructive behaviors were uncovered - my reluctance to be vulnerable and express love to my family and the root of the war I was in with my body.

I had been bothered for years by the fact that I cringed at the thought of hugging my parents or saying "I love you" to them. I would avoid physical and verbal affection at all costs to the very people who gave me life. I knew that I had a good childhood and felt so much guilt knowing that my parents hadn't done anything wrong to deserve so much aversion from me. I believed something was deeply wrong with me. I so badly wanted to return the love they showed me without disgust, but I couldn't. Every hug and every "I love you" felt forced. These feelings trickled into other close relationships. Hugging extended family members felt off. Expressing my deep care for my closest friends felt unnatural. The fact that I could easily hug acquaintances and the occasional stranger made me believe something was seriously wrong with me. I could light-heartedly say "I love you" to peers at school, but sincerely telling the same to a best friend was a no for me. I was incapable of developing true intimacy in relationships.

During one of my sessions with the counselor, we concluded the root of this problem began when I was around five or six years old. We discussed my recollection of being affectionate towards my parents prior to that age. I didn't discover in that session the reason my affections changed but the counselor's confidence that there was a valid reason for the shift was reassuring. She encouraged me to talk with my mom to see if she remembered anything significant that happened around that age.

When I talked to my mom, she disclosed that something traumatic from her own childhood resurfaced for her when I was around six. She said she became overly protective of me and admitted her own struggle with affection in relationships during that season. As she shared, I felt like I could finally breathe a breath of forgiveness for myself. I didn't blame her for being protective. It made sense. I was able to let go and finally see that I too wasn't at fault for how I felt around the people closest to me. I felt reassured it wasn't their fault, either. I never needed someone else to blame but realized I had subconsciously been dealing with trauma that was never mine. A weight lifted, and the discovery that there wasn't something wrong with me allowed me to see my relationships differently. My comfort in relationships didn't change overnight, but what did change drastically was the allowance I gave myself to work through my discomfort. I let go of the guilt and gave myself permission to be uncomfortable as the discomfort began to loosen. I saw how unhealed trauma can be passed on yet saw the hope for healing through the restorative power of Jesus Christ.

In another therapy session we focused on my eating disorder as well as my seemingly innate focus on and hatred for my body. It especially bothered me that my earliest memories surrounded what I hated most about my body. The fact that I was not a carefree child and was always self-conscious about how my body looked caused me a lot of sadness. I assumed because my youngest memories surrounded body image problems that it was something I was destined to struggle with for the rest of my life. Through the course of the therapist's questions, we determined that I indeed was born with the propensity to have body image problems. The therapist informed me I should speak to my mother again. This time, I was directed to ask my mom about her pregnancy with me because my therapist believed that my problems manifested in the womb. If you're skeptical at the thought of body image problems starting during fetal development, believe me, I was as well. I remembered, however, that my mom had mentioned previously about her own body image problems, so I thought asking her was worth a shot.

When we spoke, I again felt a sense of relief that something wasn't wrong with me. I started to see how biologically we can be wired a certain way but recognized that just because we are more prone to certain struggles does not mean we must carry them the rest of our lives. I felt freer in that moment in my body than I had before and began to see a small glimpse of hope that I didn't have to always struggle. I started to believe that there was something deeper and something holier that defined me.

Throughout that summer of therapy, I was living back at home again. I graduated with a bachelor's degree and was still working at the sports bar I had worked at throughout college. I wasn't sure what was next, but I knew I needed a change and hoped to start a career helping others. I began searching the internet for jobs in California and Florida, believing that warmer weather year-round would do me well.

One day, I came across a post on Craigslist that sparked my interest. You read that right...Craigslist. The job posting was for a wilderness youth counselor position in a small town in Florida with a population of about 5,000. I'd like to defend myself by saying that Craigslist wasn't as sketchy then; however, I do find it funny that out of all the job postings I scoured, the one that stood out to me was from a non-vetted source. I also feel the need to defend myself further by saying before I applied, I ensured the job was legitimate by reviewing the company's website. I also found the job listed on other sites and determined the company was real. To me, their post on Craigslist just indicated they wanted to hire quickly.

I had anticipated the interview process would be fast and seamless but it wasn't. Several months of emailing back and forth and spaced-out phone interviews made me want to throw the towel in. I was on the verge of giving up when it was requested I come out to Florida for an in-person interview. The in-person interview was unique because it was essentially a test run. I was asked to spend a couple of nights at the camp to see if I could handle the work and to see if I seemed like a good fit for the team. The first catch was that if I was a good fit and if I accepted the job, they would ask me to start immediately. The second catch was that they required a verbal agreement to work in that position for a minimum of two years. Something inside me told me to pack my car with what I'd need for two years because I would be staying.

Packing for the interview was the most exciting and terrifying thing I had ever done. The only place I had lived besides my childhood home was about fifteen minutes down the road. So, cramming my belongings into my car for an interview 2,000 miles away (and likely not returning) was kind of crazy.

I'll never forget crossing the border to Florida. The radio began playing the song "All By Myself." I remember feeling like I was embarking on the biggest solo adventure of my life. Little did I know that this place of solitude I was entering would be a catalyst for the biggest rise and fall I would experience before God would call me back to Him again.

Uprooting: The Painful Purpose

Most of us will experience some type of uprooting during our lifetime. Sometimes, we choose to uproot, while other times, we are forced into it. Whether it be because our childhood family moved, we decided to attend college, we made a career change, or moved across the country for a relationship, we are familiar with the feeling of being plucked up from what we once knew and dropped into a completely unfamiliar place. Sometimes, the purpose of that uprooting makes sense to us quickly; sometimes, it knocks us off our feet and takes years to recover from. Occasionally, uprooting isn't a location change but looks more like "finding" or "rediscovering" ourselves in a season of independence. Our roots, having been tangled with someone else's, require being pulled up in order to discover who we truly are. Regardless, the process of uprooting comes like a force we weren't exactly prepared for. Even when our uprooting was planned, the newness feels quite aggressive. Much like the uprooting of trees in the midst of a hurricane, uprooting in our lives is the destruction of something that our lives were deeply tied to. When uprooted, we are lifted out of familiarity, often at the expense of something or someone we considered integral to our lives. It tears us away from the life we were once accustomed to.

Before I decided to drive across the country for that job interview, I was aware my life was due for a little shaking up. When I decided to pack everything I could fit into my car and leave the rest in storage, I had hopes for a brighter and healthier future, leaving the bad behind and bringing the good with me. It was time to discover who I was outside of my comfort zone. Although I welcomed change with open arms, I was unaware of how difficult the major shift would be.

When I accepted the job at the wilderness camp and began my first solo adventure at 25 years old, I felt like I was finally entering adulthood. Whether it was naivety or desperation for a change, I considered this risky move the most adult decision I had made yet. Hello Miss Independent. The morning before my interview, my mom, who had helped me drive out, had an early flight home. I pretended to be too tired to get out of bed to give her a real hug goodbye. As I lay in bed, she leaned over to hug me, and I heard her sniffling. I quietly said, "Goodbye." Had my eyes been open, she would have seen them rolling. *Ugh, of course, she's crying,* I thought. I tried to ignore the fact that I wanted to cry, too. An independent woman would not be crying in this situation. I didn't dare admit the last bit of my comfort zone was about to walk out the door. I couldn't bring myself to face the emotion of what was really happening. Little did I know I would spend the next year calling my mom every night crying and telling her, "I hate it here." So much for independence...

When my mom left me in Florida, I wasn't expecting to experience such an array of emotions. In my heart, I understood that this new experience was good for me and I wanted to be there but I continued to cling oh-so tightly to my past. I knew without a doubt there was a grand purpose in this season, yet struggled to have faith. I acknowledged God had a different plan for my life than I did, however I continued to run back to old patterns. I've experienced this discomfort and fear many times over in my life and would guess that I'm not alone in that. We are creatures of habit, and most of us find comfort in what's familiar to us. We think we thrive off the routine of what we can expect day to day and shun any changes that throw us out of balance. We are afraid of the unknown and shy away from what appears to be too risky.

Besides the need to face my problems, I learned in my great escape from Colorado to Florida that the intense discomfort of change was inevitable. In all the excitement of newness, I didn't take into account how all of the small changes would seem so big. From the time change, to replacing the license plate on my car, to starting from scratch in building new relationships, my discomfort felt scary. I wonder though, what life would have looked like if the transition into a completely new way of life had been easy. What would I have gained? Would I have lost anything? How would those around me have been affected differently? Would where I am now be any different? I believe pain in uprooting is inevitable and, in the end, beneficial when we allow ourselves to see God in it. Like food for the soul, uprooting is equivalent to growing pain for our spirits. It's a sign of the good to come.

It's not uncommon to hear stories of people being uprooted and called to something completely new by God. Their decision to move across the country is an act of obedience to something God specifically set in motion for them. In my desperation for change, I can't say without a doubt that God is the one who uprooted me to Florida. I do believe, however, that God opened the door for me to experience Him in a new way and in a new place. The problem was that, in many ways, I was still motivated by rejection, rebellion, and fear. Maybe Florida seemed more appealing because I had recently experienced so much rejection. Maybe I thought obedience would be easier if I relocated. Maybe I wasn't so much as brave in moving but more so afraid of staying. I'm not sure, but I am certain of one thing. I know God was with me throughout it all.

Rejection, rebellion, and fear are at the root of many of our problems. Even in our desire to do life well, we get tripped up by thoughts of inferiority, impatience, and worry. We self-sabotage. We dwell on worst-case scenarios and on that which contradicts God's Word. Our problems often centered around self. We spend too much time wrapped up in ourselves and too little time concerned with God's purpose. In our attempts to evade our problems, we misinterpret our eternal purpose. We get caught up in double-mindedness and postpone our obedience to avoid hardship. We are bound to encounter troubles. That is a part of life we cannot escape, but God offers a unique perspective. He wants us to trust Him with the full picture. He sees that every detail of every story holds a special purpose for eternity and asks we have hope in the hard times and faith in the unknown. He knows we want to run away from our struggles but beckons us to run to Him with them. He sees when we try to control our pain by avoiding it but asks us to face it head-on while He holds our hand through the process. God knows our fleshly frailty and offers His Holy Spirit to empower us. He is with us, and He is surely for us.

Trusting God to walk with us through problems, especially repeated ones, is so much easier said than done. We have a tendency to lose faith the longer we experience suffering. We start wondering if God has forgotten about us or if He was even there to begin with. Our expectations of healing and lack of patience for God's timing are the perfect combination for disappointment. We forget that God sees everything we don't and far too often lose sight of the bigger picture.

The counseling I had the summer before the big move to Florida provided some much needed healing but wasn't the end all be all to the problems I continued to encounter. God didn't heal me immediately following those sessions because I still had roots He was digging up. My rebellious attitude (i.e., wanting things my way) was a root that hadn't fully been dug up. Quite frankly, I still struggle with this one. I will share more about that in later chapters, but I don't want to mislead anyone into thinking the physical uprooting of my life was followed by my faithful obedience. If anything, my relocation revealed that I was looking for an easy way out. It revealed to me that, in many ways, I still lacked trust in God. I thought a fresh start was exactly what I needed to be who, deep down, I knew I was created to be. In my mind, transformation would be nearly seamless if I was away from all familiarity. Boy, was I wrong. I needed more than a fresh start. I needed Jesus, and I needed Him more than once, twice, or even three times. Jesus, day in and day out has always been what I've needed.

Relocating to Florida was painful. I had a rude awakening when I realized my problems didn't stay in Colorado, where I had hoped to leave them in my counselor's office. As I settled into my job, I quickly experienced how emotionally draining it would be. I saw that the unhealthy thought patterns I was accustomed to were an easy fallback when I was emotionally exhausted. Ironically, I was teaching different therapeutic coping methods to teenagers while I myself still struggled with the poor coping mechanisms I developed as an adolescent. This is where I believe God really moved. I was not qualified to teach proper coping when I was still trying to figure out how to work through my own junk, but God used that opportunity to teach me, the supposed teacher.

I recall one particular incident where an adjudicated fifteen-year-old girl was sentenced to the camp for therapy instead of more time in the detention center. It was immediately evident that she was not in a place to receive help. She had been causing many issues and gave me a literal run for my money. One day, she took off, sprinting down the path away from me and the other kids in our group. I didn't know anything better to do than tell the rest of the kids to run after her with me. When I tell you this girl was fast, I mean it. She could have gotten a track scholarship had she stayed in school. I would like to say we caught up with her, but the truth is she decided she had had her fun and stopped where our campsite was.

At camp, whenever a kid misbehaved, we talked through the behaviors in hopes of accomplishing some therapeutic breakthrough within the group. These types of therapeutic discussions were called "huddles." We ended up huddling for hours with this girl. We seemingly got nowhere except being stuck sitting in the dirt, hot, hungry, and with boiling emotions from some of the other girls in the group. In general, I was feeling inadequate as a youth counselor, and this situation validated that I was not succeeding. Something life-changing happened to me that night, though.

At the height of everyone's emotions and in the middle of everyone's wishes to just go to bed because we weren't getting anywhere with the girl, she began spewing off extremely hateful things about everyone, including myself. I don't remember her exact words, but I recall recognizing them because they were things I had been telling myself for years. At that moment, she was echoing aloud my self-hate, essentially confirming the terrible things I had been believing about myself. By the grace of God and some therapeutic coping skills I had picked up at camp, I heard her words and left them there where we sat. I didn't hear what she said and thought, "See, I am blankety, blank." Instead, I heard her words and thought, "These are untruths I've believed for too long." Out loud and with my head held high, I told the girl, "The words you are saying do not affect me." I was saying the words to her but speaking them to myself. I remember that day not as a day that I stood up to a fifteen-year-old girl but as a day that I stood up to myself. I had had it with the way I treated myself for the majority of my life. I was done beating myself up and would no longer take the self-abuse. So, with all the questioning and doubting if I had made the right decision to uproot to Florida, I learned a lesson that night in the dirt. We cannot run from problems that are rooted in our hearts. Regardless of when and where the triggers started, if we do not choose to face our problems head-on and as many times as it takes, they will follow us wherever we go. God doesn't cause our pain but promises to use it. He is the master of molding what was meant to kill us into the very thing that produces life. God used that situation and those words from a fifteen year old girl that night to allow me to practice speaking His truth over my life so that I may speak truth into yours. By His grace and mercy, He didn't leave me in the dirt, but lifted me out of it. He wants to do the same for you.

Uprooted With Grace and Mercy

When we have a relationship with Jesus, grace and mercy follow us wherever we go. Many times, the hardest part is allowing ourselves to truly experience His grace and mercy because of disappointment. Perhaps you left a person, place, or thing that reminds you of your inadequacies, faults, or failures. Maybe you were then left disappointed to realize that the next person, place, or thing didn't offer anything different. I get it. This is part of my story too. The good news is, God's perfect example, gives us the opportunity to rest in grace and mercy. We intended to do the right thing. We wanted to be healthier. We were seeking newness in a way we thought would better our life. There is nothing wrong with our intentions. We can have grace for ourselves in the unknown. We can lean into kindness for ourselves by paying attention to where we have a tendency towards unkindness. We can be mindful of the attitudes and thoughts that followed us that we wished hadn't. We can consider ourselves blessed to have the realization that we were desperate for newness even if we did "new" the wrong way. We can welcome learning and growth as it comes. And when we do these things, we can experience grace and mercy increasing.

Mercy is compassion when we did the best with what we could at the time. Grace is forgiveness for taking the easier way out. Mercy is a pardoning when we truly don't deserve it.

Grace is the healing God offers us. Grace and mercy were handed over to us on the cross at Calvary. Jesus died to save us from our sin and welcome us into eternity with Him. We didn't deserve the gift He so freely offered. In this life and in our failures are opportunities to see His gift daily. He is constantly acting in and through our lives on behalf of grace and mercy.

God's free gift of eternity with Him is a hard concept to grasp for those of us who tend to dwell on mistakes of the past. It's a masochistic habit to stay stuck in the memories of the muck. And unfortunately, when we do this, we tend to prolong our learning because our energy is spent feeling shame and guilt. Rather than accepting the compassion and forgiveness of our Heavenly Father, we wonder if we will ever get it right and assume we probably won't. So where can we see God's grace and mercy in our self-depreciation? We can see it in His patience. The Bible tells us, "The Lord is not slow in keeping his promise, as some understand slowness. Instead He is patient with you, not wanting anyone to perish, but everyone to come to repentance" (2 Peter 3:9). God gives us the time and space to fully grasp the vastness of His love for us that He won't rush us and won't push us into understanding anything we aren't ready for. He doesn't want any of us to miss out on the eternal purpose He has placed on our hearts.

One of the most beautiful aspects of God's grace and mercy is the freedom He provides. He doesn't force us to follow His will. He gives us the freedom to make choices even when they don't align with His will. When we face consequences of decisions outside His will, we are granted opportunities to learn lessons for ourselves and offer encouragement to others. He is always ready with the door open to welcome us back to Him. His mercies are countless and made new daily.

There is a reason mercies are made new daily. Mercies are freshly given to us each and every day because we need mercy not once, twice, or even 1000 times over. We need endless mercy. God is a just God, yet He knows that without His compassion, we would be eternally separated from Him. In His generosity, He extends grace and mercy to cover the multitudes of our sins and failures so we may experience His love and compassion. He knows we will fall and understands we will take steps back in our faith, so He stands close by and ever ready.

For those of us who know this but still struggle to identify with grace and mercy, we have the words of Jesus to speak truth over us. When Jesus called Matthew to become a disciple and follow him, He knew very well that Matthew had sold out his Jewish culture to become a tax collector. Tax collectors were known for overcharging the people and pocketing the extra money themselves. When the Pharisees saw that Jesus had called on Matthew, they questioned why He ate with "tax collectors and sinners?" Jesus reassured them He knew what He was doing, saying it is the sick, not the healthy, who need doctors. Jesus then challenged the Pharisees to understand what He meant by saying, "I desire mercy, not sacrifice. For I have not called the righteous, but the sinners" (Matthew 9:13). God knows we will continue sinning until the day we die, yet He still loves us with a love that's so great we can't fathom. He doesn't ask for our attempts at perfection. He asks for our acceptance of His free gift. So, if you are like me, a professional at misstepping and repeated back-slider, rest assured that God has always known our frailty and faults yet still welcomes us into the fullness of His grace and mercy. It's not too late.

> The steadfast love of the LORD never ceases, his mercies never come to an end; they are new every morning; great is thy faithfulness.
>
> Lamentations 3:22-23 (ESV)

Chapter 6

Where the Moss Grows

While working at the wilderness camp, my brain was still stuck in the mentality of an eating disorder. I had learned how to control my behaviors, so I appeared healthy from the outside. And physically, I was healthy. "This is the best I'll ever get to," I thought. I accepted my reality that I was meant to stay stuck in the struggle of the mental gymnastics of constantly desiring to succumb to eating disorder rules. Food was not fuel to me. Food was the best thing in life while also the worst. It was a distraction, a motivation, and always on my mind.

Thoughts of my next meals ran rampant through my head all day long. My daydreaming of what I would look like if I were emaciated seemed like normal thoughts to have first thing in the morning. I settled with the fact that I would always have the temptation to restrict or binge and purge my food. I accepted that some part of me would always want to be skin and bones. Although I knew the psychological aspect was the most tortuous part, I came to terms with the mental torment as my thorn to bear and my cross to carry. All would be well as long as I could control how my thoughts did or did not manifest physically. I could continue living my Christian life as long as I didn't give in to the temptations.

The unfortunate thing about the temptations of an addict is that when life gets tough, the temptation comes at you with full force. Without being adequately equipped, it becomes quite burdensome to carry the load of triggers. Even without actively giving in to the addiction, the constant triggers wear you down. It had been over a year since I had acted on my eating disorder and about two years since I had self-harmed. Being at the camp motivated me to stay on the up-and-up since I was working with youth who had their own struggles. It was difficult to be around the young girls who dealt with eating disorders, but I continued to push through.

As I succeeded at keeping the behaviors at bay, I became more and more frustrated with the amount of temptation I felt. My desire to self-harm became more frequent. The impulse to purge after meals began to consume my thoughts. At one point, I took a break in the bathroom after eating lunch with the intent to give in. I couldn't take the triggers any longer. Hunched over the toilet, with my finger at the back of my throat, I tried to shut off my mind.

(Cue the mental gymnastics).

This is what you want...
　Don't start it again...
　It'll make you feel better...
　You won't be able to stop....

As I pushed my finger back further, I threw up some of the water I had chugged right before entering the bathroom. I then heard footsteps of coworkers walking by. The sound of their feet hitting the floor took me out of that moment into immediate regret. I didn't want to go back to where I previously was. I didn't want to negate all the work I had done with the counselor or all the healthy choices I had been making. My face in the toilet was the exact opposite of what I had hoped for in my life. I stood up, rinsed my mouth, washed my hands, and wiped my face. As I opened the door, I had no idea what would come in the following months. I knew that though a part of me still wished to have completed the task I set out for upon entering the bathroom, I was glad I decided to walk away from what I was about to fall back into.

I didn't know that would be the last time I'd be intentionally bent over the toilet in such a way. I didn't know that the choice to get up, walk out, and shut the door was a crucial step I needed to take towards the finality of my desire to purge. I still wholeheartedly believed I would forever be a victim of my own disordered thoughts. Not long after, I was talking to someone about how I knew I would always struggle in this way. The response I received was much like the acceptance I had already personally gained. There was no questioning whether I wanted something different, no challenge to change my perspective, and no encouragement for hope. I was not alone in my acceptance, and I was okay with that because I didn't need convincing otherwise.

A couple of months later, while on a four-hour drive, I had an encounter with the Holy Spirit that changed my perspective. I hadn't been praying for healing. I hadn't begged God to take away my temptations to restrict and purge. I was merely in the middle of worshiping God in the car when the thought of my eating disorder crossed my mind. It was a brief thought about how this struggle of mine was temporary because, in heaven, I would no longer experience it. I looked forward to that day to come. I yearned for that day to come. I had hope for that day to come. As the thought crossed my mind, I felt my hope move from my head into my heart. I felt the Lord impress upon me that He wanted to heal me in this lifetime of all aspects of my eating disorder. Instead of questioning and doubting (as I had been all along), the Spirit moved my heart in a way I never expected. I believed what God was telling me at that moment. I had confidence that He was moving. I had a new hope that didn't need to wait until I took my last breath. I had hope then and there that God's promise for me was a miraculous healing in this lifetime from over a decade of struggling. With my hands off the steering wheel (a real-life "Jesus, take the wheel" moment) and arms lifted high, I began sobbing in gratitude for what I knew in my heart that God was doing. I didn't know when I would finally feel healed, but it didn't matter because I trusted in God in a way I hadn't before.

Pruned

When we decide to follow Christ, we are laying down our old self and welcoming who we were created to be, Imago Dei, the image of God. We accept that we are imperfect people in need of a Savior. We acknowledge that Christ's offer of salvation came on the cross when He died for our sins. When we receive the salvation offered to us, the Bible tells us our old self has been crucified with Christ, and it is Christ, not us, who lives in us (Galatians 2.20 NLT). By this, we know we were created and called to be like Him. We know that by our decision to accept salvation, the old us is gone, and we are made new (2 Corinthians 5:17 NLT). Although we have not fully been sanctified in the sense of no longer sinning, the minute we accept Christ, our heart begins to change. Though we have the assurance that a simple "yes" to God changes us, we are still at odds with our flesh until the day we die. Our flesh and the

Spirit desire contrary things and remain at conflict within us (Galatians 5:17 NLT).

Transformation does not happen overnight. It is a process we begin as we come to know God more. Many people describe a shift that happens when they sincerely surrender their lives to God. I say "sincerely" because many of us grew up in the church and were taught what reflected God and what did not. We had head knowledge of what a Christian life looked like but didn't necessarily experience a shift in our own hearts' desires until much later.

No matter how fast or how slow God works to change us, it is inevitable we will notice the shift. Sometimes, He starts with the music we love. It begins to sound different, and our spirit begins to feel uneasy when we hear certain familiar lyrics that never used to bother us. Sometimes God starts by giving us new eyes to see the people we spend the most time with in a different light. We realize that their presence leaves us feeling clouded with darkness when our soul craves to be filled with light. Or God may change our opinion of how we are making money. He may reveal that the business we are in is not pleasing to Him or that the amount of focus on personal success is not His will. Maybe it's an addiction that God wants out of our life first so we can be in the right mind to comprehend His calling to serve. God's place and pace is individual to each of us. God doesn't just create us uniquely but also changes us uniquely. He knows exactly what is needed to bring us closer to Him.

Getting closer to God is His plan for us. We are here on Earth to love God fully with our heart, mind, and soul (Matthew 23:37 ESV). We do this as worship by living our lives sacrificially (Romans 12:1). John 15 uses imagery from nature to paint a beautiful picture of how the Father, the gardener, uses pruning to fulfill His plan. In the passages before, Jesus reminds us about His role in salvation. "I am the way and the truth and the life. No one comes to the Father except through me" (John 14:6 ESV). He promises the presence of the Holy Spirit upon His death to help us (John 14:25 ESV). Jesus then says He is the vine, we are the branches, who without Him, cannot do anything (John 15:5 ESV). Christ is at work in us in order to fulfill the fruitful plan for our lives. Apart from Him, we can't bear fruit. Remaining in Christ is essential to our purpose. Jesus then warns that if we do not remain in Him, we are like a dead branch thrown into the fire to be burned (John 15: 5-6 ESV). He is warning us that making a superficial commitment to follow Him is not the way to go and will have consequences.

I love the imagery of pruning trees in comparison to our spiritual walks. The entire purpose of pruning a tree is to remove the unhealthy or dead parts so that its strength is maximized and potential for further disease or pests is minimized. Removing the damaging pieces makes a much more welcoming environment for flowers and fruits to grow. With more flowers and fruits, trees are a better source of nutrients for wildlife to thrive. This is much like our potential to impact those around us. It is necessary for the cutting off of the unhealthy parts of us in order for our potential growth to be maximized. When the fruits of our spiritual pruning thrive, we become a much more welcome place for those around us to experience Jesus.

Another reason pruning trees is important is for safety. Limbs that are rotting and weak are potentially dangerous as they are much more susceptible to fall. Similarly, our lack of pruning can be extremely harmful. It's no fault of the Gardener when our stubbornness gets in the way of His pruning. When we know we are being called to live differently but refuse to obey we are harming ourselves and those around us. Sadly we see it often in church. It's quite common to meet people who claim to follow Christ but spend their weekends getting drunk and having sex outside of marriage. We see it in arrogant church leaders who belittle their spouses. We even see it in ourselves at times. It is not uncommon and that is why it's important to be attentive to the work of God. Without obedience in the pruning of the Holy Spirit, we become a danger to those around us.

Remaining in Christ, or "abiding" in Him, is essential to recognizing the work that God wants to do in us. Abiding means to "stay" or "remain stable". We do this by investing in our relationship with Christ. When we are not intentional to continue deepening our relationship with Him, we are prone to forget God's Word and promises. In turn, we are more likely to live according to our own will. Abide also means to "wait and endure". Living our lives to honor God is no easy task. We need patience in order to face the difficulties that come with following Christ. Paul reminds us though that we have a Helper. We are to walk by the Spirit, so we will not gratify the cravings of our flesh (Galatians 5:16 NKJV). Walking by the Spirit comes with knowing God more. The more time we put into learning who God is and who we are in Him, the easier it is to recognize the prompting of the Holy Spirit. This does not mean we will always do everything perfectly. However, it does create a richer environment where we experience the goodness of God through our obedience in a more tangible way.

> "My sheep hear my voice, and I know them, and they follow me"
>
> — John 10:27-28 NKJV

Life in Death

After that car ride where I had felt God's promise to heal me in this lifetime of my eating disorder, I was struggling again to believe him. A few weeks had passed, and I didn't see much change in the way my thoughts were; I began wondering if what I had heard was accurate. *Does He really want to heal me in this lifetime?* I wasn't doing anything differently besides praying more often to God with a welcome and grateful heart for Him to move. I wasn't even asking God specifically to move into that area of my life. One day, I decided to go for a walk on a trail I frequently visited. It was a relatively short path that weaved throughout a wooded area canopied by large oak trees. Right before making my way through the tree-covered path, I felt the gentle presence of the Holy Spirit. I quietly said, "Spirit, lead me."

As I began walking forward, a feeling of newness covered me. I took notice of the surrounding woods in a way I hadn't before. As if a veil was being lifted, I continued moving in anticipation. I asked, "God, what do you want to show me?" My heart welcomed whatever He wanted me to see. Peace surrounded me. I looked to my right, and a ways away, I saw several very large trees that had fallen over. I looked to my left and saw another. The way the trees were broken off on the bottom with the remainder of the tree trunk and limbs sprawled in front made it look like the trees were bowing down in worship...

"...Then shall all the trees of the forest sing for joy"

— Psalm 96:12 ESV

It was as if the Bible was coming to life before me.

I had heard the verses about how nature responds to God and had sung worship songs referencing those verses but had never seen it with my own eyes. The birds chirping in the trees, the sun peeking through the leaves, and the trees bowing down. I had never noticed such a beautiful display of worship in nature. As I continued to take note of the awe around me, my heart began to flutter. I felt God tugging. "What is it you want to show me?" I asked again, not in an attempt to rush God but to express my heart was open to whatever He wanted me to see. I continued moving, willing and ready. I began to walk ahead but felt the Spirit prompt me to proceed slowly. As I slowed, I felt impressed upon to walk even slower. I slowed my pace, and again, I felt the prompt, "slower." I was nearly standing still when I felt like the Lord asked me to kneel down in the middle of the path. "What if someone sees me?" I prayed aloud. Again, I had the prompting to kneel down right there. In obedience, I knelt down for some time and felt a peace rest over me. I had no idea why I was being asked to kneel in the middle of the path, but felt confident in my submission.

After a little while, I felt released to stand back up. As I rose to my feet, I felt another prompt to step off the path a little ways. As I moved forward, my eyes drew me to a small area. Normally, I wouldn't pay it mind, but I knew God was leading me there. I took one intentional step after another until I saw a tree stump right in front of me. I couldn't take my eyes off it. It had clearly been dead for a while. The tree that had been attached was nowhere to be found. As I continued to observe the tree stump, I noticed the most vibrant green moss covering the rotted edges atop it. At that moment, I felt God saying to me, "There is life in death." Tears filled my eyes as I realized He wasn't just talking about the tree stump. He was talking about the life that was to come with the death of my eating disorder. He reiterated the promise of being healed in this lifetime by reassuring me that life was to come from it. He wasn't done with me, but death had to come first. I left the woods that day filled with an unexplainable hope. I knew there would be obstacles to overcome, but realized that God was right there, walking me through them.

It wouldn't be long before I got to experience the freedom of God's promise. There was a health and wellness event at work where a team of nurses came to educate and evaluate us. I was fine with being weighed but specifically requested my weight be kept from me. The risk of hearing a number I didn't like and taking it to an unhealthy place was too much...so I thought.

As the nurse shared my results with me, she forgot my request and told me my weight. I sat there a little taken aback that my attempt to protect myself wasn't respected. Upon hearing how much I weighed, I had an almost out-of-body experience where I was looking down at myself and into my brain. I could see the number and two paths ahead of the number. One path was a path of familiarity. It's where I could see my weight, think about it the rest of the day, then decide which restrictive or purging action I wanted to take. The other path was foreign to me. I couldn't see where it led but I knew it was different because that number had no place on it. I knew I had a decision to make at that moment.

I decided to take the latter route. I heard my weight as a number that held no value. It didn't consume my thoughts nor did it determine my day's outcome. It was just a number. I wish I could bottle up the feeling of freedom and empowerment I felt at that moment. I left that meeting with the nurse feeling light and strong. For the first time, I experienced what it means to walk in freedom. For the first time, I understood how life can come from death.

Is there anything God is currently revealing to you that

needs to be put to death so life can spring forth? Where does He want you to experience new life through His freedom? The truth is that we all will continue to have things that need to die in order to experience life in Christ. Whether we are currently aware of what needs to be put to death or not, we can be certain that God is still working. Maybe that excites you. Maybe that scares you. Wherever you find yourself, be encouraged that God knows what He is doing.

Mossy Lessons

What I love about reflecting on God's testimony from this time in my life are the lessons I see repeated and the permanent change I see He's done in me through those lessons. The process of life coming from death. This story from my life is just one example out of an innumerable amount of stories from countless people who have encountered the same lessons. Stories upon stories just go to show the consistency of God and the power of prayer.

God doesn't want us to be passive followers. He wants us actively engaged in what He is doing.

In Philippians, we see Paul's encouragement to pray and petition God in *all* things (ESV). Paul instructs the church of Colossae to be devoted in prayer (Colossians 4:2). Paul continues his instructions to pray in 1 Thessalonians and says prayer is the will of God. There is a distinct aspect of prayer that Paul is calling the church to in each of these references we cannot ignore- gratitude. His encouragement is to pray about everything, pray continuously, and *pray with thanksgiving*.

The thing about gratitude is that it changes the way we perceive our circumstances. Being thankful in everything allows us to experience peace about our prayers we likely wouldn't be able to otherwise. The difference of a prayer with and without gratitude can change the trajectory of what we learn in our circumstances. For example, when I first began praying about my self-harm, I was pleading with God to take the pain away. I wanted Him to put a stop to it right then and there. Though I believe I was doing the best I knew how to at the time, I see that years later, as my prayers began to shift towards gratitude, the outcome of my circumstances became less pressing and less cumbersome. I never stopped hoping for a way out, but my prayers changed from a request to be rescued to searching for what God was doing through my pain.

The second lesson I've taken from God's work in my life is the importance of having an open heart. God wants us to be open and honest in our prayer life with Him. Like Job, a man in the Bible described as "righteous," who began questioning God when his life shifted from having everything to having nothing, God desires our honesty in every situation. Job spent a lot of time in turmoil, received counsel from friends, and continued to cry out to God. Throughout Job's prayers, he wrestled to understand what God was doing, and in the end, his questioning led to humility. "Surely I spoke of things I did not understand, things too wonderful for me to know" (Job 40:3). Job didn't get a full understanding of his situation, but he appeared to become more open to God's plan in the end.

God wants our willingness to allow Him to be the Lord of our life. In our prayers, our willingness to be moved by God ends up transforming us. Our willingness doesn't always come automatically, though. Sometimes, we need to sit with our questions for some time before relinquishing them to God in trust. Sometimes, we need to experience the consequences of our own stubbornness and unbelief to grasp how much greater God is. I have experienced many changes of heart as I continued to pray repeatedly about something. A certainty I had that God would answer my prayer in a way that made sense to me and in a timeframe that made sense to me transformed into a trust that His way transcends all constraints I had. Oftentimes, we want rescuing and immediate answers, but God's work in the waiting is amazing. He begins to change our hearts and reveal the ways we've been hanging on to control. He beckons us to release control to Him. With softened hearts, when we choose to release control, we are handing over responsibility. We are opening our hands to Him, saying, "Here, God, it's yours. Do as you please."

Something amazing happens when we pray with open hands. God frees us from our rigid ways of thinking and believing and opens up a new way to experience Him. His love, freedom, strength, and greatness abound when we move out of the way. When we remove timeframes and ultimatums from our prayers, our hearts become more willing for whatever may come.

Equally, I've learned that it is good to be expectant of God and with Him in our prayers. It is the trust that God is who He says He is and the hope that He will do what He has promised. Having an expectant heart is sincere anticipation to see God move. Expectancy is best experienced when our "why" is to honor God, and we leave the "what, when, where, and how" up to Him. We may have in mind exactly what we want to bring to God, but in prayer, God may reveal something different to focus on. For instance, we may pray about a job change with the idea that God is calling us into something different. However, throughout those prayers, we discover it's not a new job God is calling us into but a new attitude about the same job. Or maybe a new job is what God is calling us into, but His time frame to transition us takes much longer than we're comfortable with. The "where" could look like Him keeping us at the same company but on a new team, or it could be the same job in a new location. God's "how" could look like failed job interview after failed job interview, followed by our obedience to stop at a specific coffee shop only to happen to run into the CEO of a startup company.

The ways God moves are countless, and yet what He really only asks from us is to come to Him with open hands.

Another lesson is that God's pace is the right pace. I look back at that walk through the woods and can't help but smile at just how slow I was walking at one point. It felt like I was actually about to start walking backwards. I think God moves like that sometimes. He is slow with intention. His pace is purposeful so we don't miss anything and so that what we face isn't too abrupt. If I had been walking any faster, chances are I would have missed His prompt to walk into the area off-path. I would have missed the tree stump if I had not walked into that area. Without seeing the tree stump, I would have missed out on a tangible example of life growing out of something dead.

He knew what He was doing, just like He always does. His pace and His way aren't just about us either. We tend to forget how our stories are all intertwined into one grand picture God has painted. His timing in our individual lives is about the bigger picture. Accepting God's pace is accepting God's plan. 2 Peter 3:8-9 tells us that time to us is vastly different from how God views time; "with the Lord one day is as a thousand years, and a thousand years as one day." This verse also tells us the Lord is not slow but rather patient with us because He wants us all to come to know Him (NKJV).

My favorite and hardest lesson of all is that God isn't done. Jesus stated, "My Father is always working and so am I" (John 5:17). We can see this in our own lives over time in how we become sanctified. Sanctification is the process of becoming holy as well as the declaration of naming something holy. When we accept Christ as our Savior, we are declared sanctified and considered holy by His blood. At the same time, we enter into a process of becoming like Christ and, therefore, holier through the Holy Spirit. God has continued to use His promise and process of healing from different seasons of my life. The lessons I have taken with me are lessons I continue to learn more through.

The day in the woods wasn't the last time God would use moss to speak to me about life in death. That day with the nurses wasn't the last time God would unchain me and walk me through temptation with the freedom He offers. These moments stand as beautiful reminders that God isn't done yet because He is a God of completion. The Bible tells us that God is a God who finishes what He starts. God continues to work out His plan in us (Philippians 1:6 NKJV).

If you are having difficulty seeing God in your situation, keep praying. Keep releasing your burdens to Him every minute, every second of the day. Expect God to work in your life. Open your heart to allow God to move in *His way* and in *His time,* and if you're struggling with this one, tell God! Like a father asking for healing for his son, "Lord I believe, help my unbelief!" (Mark 9:24 NKJV). The prayer can be simple and needs to be honest. Finally, meditate on His Word day and night.

> "For the word of God is living and active, sharper than any two-edged sword, piercing to the division of soul and of spirit, of joints and of marrow, and discerning the thoughts and intentions of the heart."
>
> — Hebrews 4:12 ESV

Chapter 7

A Wolf in Sheep's Clothing

I've always found it interesting how quickly we lose trust in God's plan. In our walk with God, we experience something incredible, even miraculous, only to find ourselves back to questioning His faithfulness. This is exactly what happened to me after seeing God work the miracle of healing me from an eating disorder and self-harm.

I was in a much better place mentally and spiritually when my focus started to shift increasingly toward my desire for marriage. Marriage and having a family were experiences I knew I wanted to have since childhood. I played "wedding" almost daily as a child and treated my dog like my baby, wrapping her in blankets and rocking her to sleep in my doll's cradle. In middle school, I was in a Bible study where my leader told us about how God answered her prayers for a godly spouse. So, at 13 years old I began praying for a spouse. In high school, I thought I would marry my first boyfriend, and when we broke up less than two years later, I continued my search for my future spouse. Every guy friend, every crush, and every boyfriend became a potential spouse...and there were lots of them. I was so focused on marriage in college that I ignored a sea of red flags in hopes God would work a miracle. After college and after experiencing a season of promiscuity, I took a break from dating and was okay with focusing on myself because I knew I really needed to get healthier. My goal was to be in a better spot personally so I would be better prepared to become a spouse. I knew my mental health needed to be a priority before another person could be. Sadly, as I experienced redemption in one area of my life, sin, and idolizing marriage began to take over in a way I never expected.

I had been at my job for over a year and developed strong bonds with my coworkers. We were with each other 24/7. They had become like a second family. On my days off, I tried to find churches to connect with other believers. I found a church, and for about six months, I succeeded in having friends outside my job. I would drive an hour and a half any Tuesday night I was off to attend a young adult's group. On other days off, I would hang out with the group of people I connected with at whatever gatherings or meetups they had planned. I found myself attracted to a couple of the guys, and it was exciting to know that there were Christian men nearby.

One guy in particular caught my eye and we started talking more often. Like the pattern I was prone to, my heart jumped ahead, hoping he could be *the guy*. I quickly gave him too much attention and soon found myself in a precarious situation with him at his home one night. I slept over at his house, and though nothing besides kissing happened, I knew in my heart that a boundary had been crossed. I had given him more of myself than he had shown he was worthy of having. As dramatic as that sounds, I knew in my heart that I was giving him the wrong impression about myself by staying over and starting a physical relationship before really getting to know him better. I so badly wanted to make up for my mistake that I leaned in even more, trying to get close to this guy. He sent many signals that he was losing interest, but I ignored them and continued to find opportunities to be in his presence, hoping he would fall in love with me and that we would live happily ever after. My habit of hoping for a miraculous change of his heart in the midst of my lack of self-control and trust in God led me to embarrassment once again.

I told my mom about this guy, repeatedly mentioning my attraction to him, and she offered encouragement by saying she believed God had someone for me but that I needed to be open to whoever it may be. "Who knows? Maybe He's got someone you typically aren't physically attracted to," she said. That statement was etched in my brain. Part of me hoped what she said wasn't true, while the other part of me knew it could be a good idea not to be so picky about physical attractiveness.

One night, I was telling my friend and coworker about the guy I liked. I told her how he'd been acting a little distant, but I still hoped something could come of it. She responded, "I don't think he's good enough for you. I think you deserve someone who wants to care for you and will love you." The tone of her voice was more than comforting. Her response seemed inviting and slightly flirtatious, as if she was offering to take on responsibility that the guy evidently was not. It made me uncomfortable and, at the same time, a little curious.

Was she talking about herself? I wondered. *Surely not...but it kind of sounded like she was insinuating herself...*

I shook off my thoughts and redirected the conversation quickly. I wasn't attracted to women and, regardless, grew up believing women weren't supposed to date each other. There was no reason for me even to consider her as anything but a friend. Besides, she was sort of like a sister to me.

I happened to be off work the next couple of days and was

left to fight off my questions about her statement. I couldn't help but wonder what she meant when she gave me her opinion of what I deserved in a relationship. My desire to be deeply loved welcomed what her statement seemed to suggest, while my opinions about same-sex relationships wanted no part in thinking further about it.

Over those next few days, I did my best not to think about my friend and made poor attempts at chalking up my growing questions as *nothing to worry about*. Despite my attempts to evade gay thoughts and curiosities, my questions invaded my sleep one night. I had a dream about her. I frequently dreamt about my job and my coworkers, but this wasn't just any dream. This dream highlighted my friend in an unexpected way, and in the dream, it was evident we had mutual feelings for each other.

Although I woke up knowing that it was just a dream, I couldn't shake how I felt towards my friend in that dream. I had never had feelings like this about other friends I dreamt about. It was clear that my curiosities were turning into actual feelings, and my dream reiterated it all. Truthfully, I found it disturbing and quite disruptive to everything I once knew about myself. *Why did I have this dream? I'm not attracted to her, am I? I'm not a lesbian. And if I'm not, why do I feel the way I do about her?* I had often joked about being a lesbian or having a male body part, but never once did I consider myself anything but straight. Now that I had these feelings about my friend that made me uncomfortable, I became entirely confused.

Counterfeits

It's not a secret that Satan hates the good work of God in our lives. He despises nothing more than a Christian who is seeking and following the Lord's plan for his or her life. When we are genuinely after the Lord's will, we can expect Satan and his team of demons to work overtime to throw us off course. Temptation, doubt, distraction, lies, shame, and guilt from sin are a few of the tactics he uses to turn us away from God. He knows the temptations of our flesh. He's a master at observing our downfalls and weak points.

Even when we are not engaging in deliberate sin, he has evil schemes that appear to be the opposite. He will introduce false gospels packaged nicely and tickle our desire to feel good. Paul, warning the church of Corinth of false teachers, points out that Satan "transforms himself into an angel of light" (2 Corinthians 11:14 NKJV). Society has wrapped up messages of social justice, love, prosperity, and personal success as the "Christian thing to do," and Satan thrives off of it. He uses our desire to do good for others and our want to feel purpose as a means of diversion. Feeling purposeful and doing good aren't bad things when anchored in truth. It's crucial to know, however, that the purpose of a true Christian life is centered on doing good in the sight of God rather than the world. We often fall into the trap of feeling comforted by doing what other people view as the right thing. The truth is that following Christ is often very uncomfortable because of its requirement of sacrifice. We are called to deny ourselves, carry our cross, and follow Him (Matthew 16:24 NKJV). That means there is a heavy burden in following Christ; we are required to give up our fleshly desires to honor God.

The devil wants us to believe that discomfort is wrong. He wants us to fall into the comfort that comes with constantly seeking "what I want" via prosperity and personal success. He wants us to desire our own happiness over God's holiness. He wants us to seek success in worldly things and has a way of manipulating us into believing that a life of comfort is the goal. And we love to believe that comfort and success are the top goals in life.

Even in our Christian faith, we want to feel like we are succeeding at being "good Christians," and we love to talk about our "blessings" in terms of monetary provision and health. Our prayers are about what we can receive from God instead of what He wants us to sacrifice. We easily fall for the lie that comfort is the way of life and that we must avoid discomfort at all costs. We see this in how Peter responded to Jesus' acknowledgment of His impending sacrifice. Peter was so uncomfortable with the thought that Jesus would soon face a brutal death in Jerusalem that he challenged Jesus, saying that would never happen to him. Jesus knew the truth and immediately called out Peter's false claim, saying he did not have the will of God in mind (Mathew 16:21-23 NKJV). If we aren't careful to seek truth in all things, we are prone to fall for the schemes of Satan. We are prone to avoid sacrifice and to question God when life becomes uncomfortable.

Because comfort is such a temptation for us, counterfeits are the perfect tactic Satan uses against the person whose heart's desire is to follow God. With our inclination to desire blessings to come in the form of financial stability, a spouse, or fame, we are subject to deceit by counterfeits. Sometimes God does provide blessings in these ways. Satan wants us to expect that type of blessing and to doubt God when a blessing comes in a package that isn't so shiny. So, Satan and his demons will disguise themselves and their schemes to look like they are from God to trick us. If he can package something nicely that looks like it could be from God, and we don't do our due diligence to check its validity in Christ, we risk falling for his scheme. Satan is thrilled any time we believe his scheme is actually God-sent. Take religion, for example. Satan knows we were created to be made complete in God. He sees our desire to live with a higher purpose in life and uses false religion to his advantage. When we follow false gods or twist the Christian faith to suit our desires, he is pleased to leave us to our own demise.

We have the responsibility to take all things to God. Test our faith by prayer, fasting, and reading God's word. Receiving counsel is also important, but I would argue that counsel is a good supplement to others rather than a replacement. If we spend our time only discovering our faith through the lenses of pastors and church leaders we look up to, we are impairing our ability to communicate directly with God. Though God uses people in our lives to speak to us, He wants us to know Him through His Word. Much like His promise to the Israelites in exile, "Then you will call upon me and come and pray to me, and I will hear you. You will seek me and find me when you seek me with all your heart" (Jeremiah 29:12-13 ESV). God desires an authentic relationship with each of us.

"Love is love" was a counterfeit ideology I fell for in my attraction to my friend. I started to close myself off from relationships I knew would challenge that ideology and began looking to people who I knew welcomed same-sex relationships. Although I wasn't openly discussing my curiosity with anyone else, I was observing those around me. I started looking at romantic relationships between women and noting all the things I really admired about how they treated each other. In my experience with guys, I didn't get the empathy, understanding, love, and support that was so evident in the lesbian relationships I was witnessing. I began to question why such loving relationships would be considered a sin when they appeared much healthier than the majority of heterosexual relationships I had been around. I began to question what I had been taught in church and wasn't sure where I stood any longer on my view of same-sex relationships as a sin. Previously, it hadn't been something I paid much mind to because I hadn't been around many gay people. I surely hadn't been attracted to a woman before.

When I began experiencing curiosity and questions for myself, my beliefs became quite muddled. I wanted answers and sought every justification possible from those around me. *Why was I suddenly experiencing romantic feelings for another woman?* My mom's comment about me possibly ending up with someone I wouldn't normally be attracted to kept popping into my mind as I pondered my growing feelings for my friend. I knew my mom didn't intend to direct me toward a relationship with another woman. Still, I subconsciously twisted the knowledge that God uses other people to speak to us and thought maybe her statement was a sign I should try something or, rather, someone new I wouldn't have considered before. I didn't consider the thought of counterfeits because, truthfully, I didn't know scripture that well. I could've opened my Bible. I chose instead to look for other people to help answer my questions. I also didn't consider my sudden curiosity and increasing time spent pondering the idea to be wrong. With that, the more time I spent thinking about my feelings and thinking about her, I justified it as trying to figure out where I stood on it being a sin issue. My growing feelings weren't hurting anyone, so I thought.

Our feelings are the perfect gateway for Satan to introduce his counterfeits. He has a way of seducing us into believing that what we desire is always good and that we are deserving of experiencing those desires. Sometimes, he influences us with the thought that *our desire isn't hurting anyone else* and, therefore, is justified. Other times, he doesn't have to do any work because we are the ones doing the justifying. Logically, we know there is no such thing as a harmless sin, but our actions justify them as such. The seemingly harmless sin is the sneakiest and arguably the deadliest sin because it's so closely linked to pride. Most of us have explained away our wrongdoings with "it's not hurting anyone" or "the only one I'm hurting is myself." These are merely poor excuses to avoid admitting the truth of our choices. Once we've acted on our desires, we've opened the door for more sin. Eventually, we are left to face reality; what once seemed benign turned into a cancer capable of killing us.

> Lust is the devil's counterfeit for love. There is nothing more beautiful on earth than a pure love and there is nothing so blighting as lust.
>
> — D.L. Moody

Footholds

We are especially prone to falling for counterfeits when we have given Satan a foothold in our lives. A "foothold" is "a position usable as a base for further advance."[1] In the Christian life, this means there is something set in our life with wrong intentions or beliefs that is at risk of becoming progressively more dangerous to us. Footholds are not often a deliberate choice we make but rather what happens when we lack faith in a certain area. If we do not completely trust God in all things, we are in jeopardy of giving the devil an opportunity to take hold. Harboring unforgiveness, giving in to distractions, ignoring convictions, forgoing repentance, having idols, and remaining stagnant are all ways we can open the door to footholds.

My idolization of marriage and blindspots in relationships were the exact footholds Satan needed to pull me further from God's plan in my life. Because I doubted God's provision in the area of marriage, I made myself an easy target. It wasn't just evident in my feelings towards my female friend either. Satan had that foothold long before in all of my ungodly romantic relationships. I was willing to ignore red flags, loosen boundaries, and make attempt upon attempt to justify unholy relationships as potentials for godly marriages. The number of times I thought I was capable of influencing a guy to become a man of God amidst my loose physical boundaries and despite his clear sexual motivation is embarrassing. I constantly traded faith that God would provide for fear that I would be lonely forever. In that fear, I repeatedly stepped in where I should have stepped aside for God to do a good work in and through me.

Surprisingly, I did pray about marriage frequently. My prayers, however, were always centered around me and my desires. I prayed about what *I* wanted God to give *me* in a spouse and in marriage. Any offerings in my prayers were half-hearted requests for God to change my desire to be married if it wasn't His will, followed up with more prayers about my hopes and plans. Honestly, I didn't want God to change my desire to be married because I didn't trust His plan.

The unfortunate reality is that our desires, when left unsubmitted to the Lord day in and day out, incline us towards open doors for the devil. The only real way to combat his evil plans is to constantly seek the Lord with hands open, believing and trusting that God truly knows best. In Ephesians, Paul calls believers to live redeemed and to leave behind our old selves (Ephesians 4:22 ESV). He reminds us we were previously ruled by our desires in this world, and our redeemed selves have eternity set in our hearts, motivating us daily to discover what God wants to use us for. Paul warns believers not to give Satan an opportunity (Ephesians 4:27 ESV). When we give the devil a foothold in our lives (meaning our heart is set on worldly things), we are ultimately giving him the opportunity to take us in the opposite direction of God.

Course Correction

Our greatest tools against Satan's plans are written out for us in scripture. First and foremost, acknowledging and accepting the gift of Christ's salvation is necessary. Ephesians 2:8-9 tells us there is nothing of ourselves or our efforts that save us - it is the gift of God's grace through faith that frees us (NKJV). Without receiving Christ as our Savior, we do not have the miraculous power of the Holy Spirit within us that frees us from our former enslavement to sin (Romans 8 NKJV). When we live by the Spirit, we are capable of fighting off Satan's schemes and instead engage in course correction. Course correction is about allowing the Lord, rather than our own hearts, to direct our steps (Proverbs 16:9 NKJV). There are many ways He will correct and direct our paths.

His Word gives us hope that we are capable, through Him, to overcome that which tends to ensnare us and impair us in our faith:

Forgive.

If we are harboring unforgiveness, we must forgive (Mark 11:25; Ephesians 4:32; Matthew 18:21-22 ESV). Forgiveness is paramount to practice over and over because it is a fundamental aspect of the Christian faith. Without Christ's forgiveness, we are dead to our sins. Life flows abundantly out of living in the forgiveness we were granted at Calvary. We are called to forgive, just as Christ forgave us. When we act on the call to forgive, we are closing the door for Satan's scheme of bitterness, self-righteousness, and hate to grow. Forgiveness is described as "a conscious, deliberate decision to release feelings of resentment or vengeance toward a person or group who has harmed you, regardless of whether they deserve your forgiveness."[2] This is different from reconciliation. We are not always called to reconciliation, but we are always called to forgiveness.

Stay vigilant.

We are instructed to steer clear of the distractions of this world (Proverbs 4:25-27; Mark 4:19; Ephesians 5:15-16 ESV). When our hearts are turned towards eternity, we have a hedge of protection against the innumerable distractions Satan would love for us to fall for. The world around us doesn't hold as much weight because we know it is temporary. With our sights set on things above, any distraction the devil attempts to steer us away with is powerless. This is a minimalist life. By holding only what adds value and meaning to our lives and those around us, our time and energy spent are much more productive. Limiting distractions can look like putting our phones and computers away more often, investing most of our time in a few core relationships in our lives that are life-giving, and opening our Bible first before looking for advice from pastors or podcasts we enjoy. Essentially, limiting distractions requires setting healthy boundaries.

Listen to convictions.

We must heed convictions and repent to carry out the works God has called us to (John 13:19-21; 1 John 1:9; 2 Corinthians 7:9-10 ESV). As believers, we are being transformed and renewed daily. It is our job to listen to the workings of the Holy Spirit in our lives. That little feeling you get before you say something you shouldn't? God gives us that as an opportunity to do our part in becoming more like Him. The temporary nature of this world does not give us an excuse to avoid repentance. Though grace is given freely to those who accept it, the sincerity of our faith is evident by our fruit. If we call ourselves Christian but never implement repentance in our lives, chances are the heart never truly changed. If we find ourselves with a calloused heart, it's time we ask the Holy Spirit to work in us and show us what we need to turn from. Praying for conviction can be scary; however, the mercy and redemption that come with repentance are astounding.

Act in faith.

Moving forward in our faith rather than remaining stagnant is vital. Faith keeps us moving ahead in God's plan (2 Corinthians 5:7 ESV). Growing in our faith is equivalent to knowing God more. We are instructed to grow in grace and knowledge (2 Peter 3:18 ESV) We do this by fellowship with other believers, stepping out in faith, and practicing our gifts. (1 Timothy 1:6; Hebrews 10:25; 1 Peter 4:10 ESV). Instead of being indifferent or apathetic, we are to be zealous and fervent in our faith, having a passion for what the Lord is doing. The devil wants us to be complacent and often disguises it in our comfort. This looks a lot like being a lukewarm Christian, which the Bible warns us about (Revelation 3:15- 16 ESV).

Lose the idols.

Letting go of idols is imperative. We are told to flee from idols (1 Corinthians 10:14 ESV). We are told to put our idols to death (Colossians 3:5 ESV). We are warned that keeping idols keeps us suffering and away from God's love (Psalms 16:4;

Jonah 2:8 ESV). There is only one true God, and we are to revere Him as such. When we hold anything, person, belief, or mindset over God, we are guilty of idolization. To relinquish idols to God is to place Him, above all else, on the throne of our lives. Satan wants that throne. God already has the throne as a whole, but we choose whether He has the throne in our lives or not. We experience His glory when we give Him the place He deserves in our lives.

Course correction is part of growing in our faith. When willing, we are in an ongoing process of sanctification that requires adjustments along the way. Course correction does not come easy.

This is another reason why abiding in Christ is necessary. When we abide, we *patiently endure* what comes with correction. That means whatever we struggle with, we must continually submit to the Lord. We do this as an act of worship and trust in God's good plan. He wants to guide us and wants to move in and through us. When we seek the Lord's correction and direction, we are saying, "Here I am, Lord. Send me" (Isaiah 6:8 NKJV). That part is scary to me because I know I'm a whole mess as is. When I welcome further corrections, I tend to brace myself. I don't typically want to learn more ways in life I can improve, and selfishly, I do not want to sacrifice the ways I am accustomed to. On the reverse side, I have never regretted being obedient to what God has called me to.

The good news is that when our heart is truly set on the Lord's will, we are naturally more open to God's correction and direction. We are also more willing to relinquish our doubts, insecurities, and fears. In turn, we get to experience the greatness of God in our submission. The power that comes from yielding to God's plan and His corrections in our lives is incomparable to anything we can do on our own. When we are chasing after the one True God by handing over our idols,

Satan is afraid of us because he knows the power we behold through Christ.

"Now to him who is able to do far more abundantly than all that we ask or think, according to the power at work within us."

— Ephesians 3:20 ESV

Chapter 8

Watering Weeds

My confusion about my feelings towards my female friend changed as soon as we both admitted to having feelings for each other. As soon as we expressed our feelings, we became inseparable. There's a common joke in the gay community about lesbians moving fast in their relationship when they start dating. The "U-Haul Effect" is used to describe women dating who have become committed to one another especially quickly. I have some thoughts on that, but I'll save them for another time. Although the female-to-female relationship was new to me, I wasn't scared about becoming so quickly connected to her. I was actually excited about it. This was the mutual relationship I had always wanted with guys and never experienced.

With a guy, I felt like I had to play some sort of game initially to keep him interested. When he showed more interest, I couldn't help but become overly eager. I wasn't good at playing the game and always made myself available whenever the guy wanted to hang out (apparently, guys don't typically appeal to the "always available" thing.) With her, there was no game. She wanted to be with me and talk to me as much as I did her. We found every excuse to be around each other as much as possible at work, and when our days off aligned, we did everything together. We were quick to put a label on our relationship with each other; however, we didn't openly share it with other people right away. She had never dated a girl before either, and it felt safer to experience something so foreign to both of us on our own for some time. She wasn't just my girlfriend. She was my best friend, and I couldn't imagine life without her. We said "I love you" to each other within the first couple of months of dating, and though it felt somewhat odd at how fast the feelings mutually grew, I loved being loved so deeply and quickly. My heart had always yearned to be cherished the way that I felt her cherish me.

Although we hadn't told anyone at work about our relationship, it became obvious something was going on because of how aggressively our "friendship" grew. Rumors started going around, and people started asking questions. When we told them, they were generally accepting. The people who were not comfortable with our relationship made it known, so we kept our distance from them. I knew my parents wouldn't understand, so I decided it was best to introduce her as my best friend, hoping they would fall in love with her without any judgment. In my mind, this would make the big reveal easier when the time came. It was quite easy to keep the relationship a secret from family and friends back home because my communication with them was far and few between. Although she wasn't as adamant about keeping us a secret from certain people as I was, she seemed to understand where I was coming from. I liked the relationship we had developed in our little bubble of support and didn't want opposing opinions to interfere.

As my relationship with her grew, the time I spent with

God became less and less. I was praying less often and wasn't reading my Bible. The bit of scripture I was exposing myself to was through short devotionals that cherry-picked one verse at a time to accompany whatever the daily topic was. I wasn't getting any sustenance. I was too busy indulging myself with whatever sounded best at the time. The depth in my relationship with God, all in all, was lacking.

I still wasn't certain where the Bible landed on homosexuality, and rather than researching scripture, I was referred to a book that claims the Bible supports same-sex relationships. I was eager to read the book and hoped to find justification for my newfound love. I desperately wanted to have her and God. I wanted this so badly that I avoided going directly to God about the matter because I was afraid of what I would find out. I knew of the verses Christians typically recited to prove God's Word doesn't align with homosexuality. I wasn't convinced though, that there wasn't some sort of translation error. As I continued to lean further away from seeking God on the matter, I continued to look to her and others around me who justified a gay Christian life. I was comforted that she said she was Christian as well. Though less experienced in all things church related, I accepted her proclamation of the Christian faith. She was a newer Christian but I believed she was sincere, and that gave me hope for the godly marriage I had always wanted.

Over time, I began feeling conviction and convinced myself it was because we had crossed physical boundaries. One night, when I was sharing how I had always wanted to wait until marriage and all of my failures to do so, she compassionately said she was willing to hold up all physical boundaries I desired until marriage. Her answer was the right answer—the answer I always wanted to hear from a guy. I should have been elated, but something about her answer concerned me. Whether I didn't believe her, didn't believe we were capable of following through, or was confused about something else, I didn't allow myself to think further about my concern. I reverted to the fact that I loved her, and she loved me. The connection, comfort, and support in our relationship was what I had always wanted. That was all that mattered.

As our bond continued to get stronger, our physical boundaries became less of a priority. I didn't feel the same conviction as I did before. We were talking about marriage, so I justified our actions. I couldn't picture my life without her. She felt the same. Our relationship was so intense that marriage naturally became a topic of conversation. The thought of marriage to her did not scare me; however, the idea of a wedding did. My parents still didn't know we were dating, and I didn't know how to tell them. Picturing a wedding with her seemed odd, but I assumed it was because of my hesitation in telling my parents. When we would talk about marriage, I challenged her on many occasions to ask herself if she was really okay with never being with a man again. She tended to take on more of the masculine role in our relationship, so I questioned if she missed being in a more feminine role. She would confirm how much she loved me and enjoyed taking care of me. Her reassurance felt nice; however, I still wondered if she felt like she was missing out. In hindsight, I believe my questions to her were really meant for me. I didn't want to admit that I struggled with the thought of walking down the aisle to her instead of a man. I loved her, and the thought of losing her devastated me.

About two years into our relationship, and after a hard conversation about the relationship still being secret from our families, we decided it was time to tell our parents. She wasn't worried about telling her parents like I was. I was mortified. The conversation with my parents went about as I expected. I felt like I had ruined my parents' lives. The conversation with her parents was much easier. They offered their support no matter who she loved. Many people would assume that her parents' response was the correct response and my parents' response was homophobic and unloving. Many people would think my parents were unfair, judgmental, and wrong to have the questions and concerns they had. I was disappointed and sad that they responded the way they did, but I understood that the way they believed they should love me was with Biblical truth. Though I wasn't sure I agreed with what they believed to be Biblical truth, I always knew my parents were doing the best they could. Even with that understanding of my parents' priority of faith, I desired less and less to be around them or have meaningful conversations with them. Being around anyone who didn't support us was rather uncomfortable, and I wanted to avoid hard conversations at all costs. I maintained a distant relationship with them, and each conversation became more surface-level than the last. In my mind, it was the way our relationship had to be. If we couldn't agree on this major aspect of my life, then there wasn't much to talk about.

There were several people in my life who felt sorry for me and were mad at the way my parents responded. I accepted their condolences but still maintained a level of respect for my parents. I didn't want others to judge my parents, but I knew that was inevitable. I saw how many people believed I should have been accepted by my parents in a very specific "love is love" kind of way. Sure, I wanted that for myself, but what bothered me the most was that my parents were missing out on a relationship with my girlfriend. I thought the world of her and wanted nothing more than to see her and my parents get along. It wasn't that they didn't get along. My parents liked her, but they liked her as my friend. Because they weren't welcoming of our relationship as it stood, I felt protective of her and continued to let the distance with my parents grow. If they weren't going to treat her like family, I didn't want to be around them much. Because of this, I entered further into a self-imposed isolation from people who didn't openly support my relationship with her. All seemed well because we had her family and our mutual friends who supported us. We also had my select group of friends from home and family whom I figured would either be supportive or wouldn't voice their opposition if they didn't agree. Despite the support from select friends and family, I still yearned for my parents' approval.

She and I decided to leave our job around the same time so we could start a new life together. We didn't have any other jobs lined up, so her family welcomed us with open arms. We started temporary jobs and lived in her family's house for a few months as we job-searched. My time there was a glimpse into what I had always hoped for from in-laws. They were all such welcoming and lovely people, making my feelings about my parents harder to deal with. I was grateful we had her family, at least. One day I received a letter from my grandmother (who was not aware of my relationship). The letter was over a page long and described her wishes for me to find a good husband. She said her dream was for all her granddaughters to experience marriage and motherhood. Ironically, her letter was written on a piece of paper with a giant rainbow around the edges. I couldn't help but think maybe it was a sign that I was in the right relationship despite her clear wishes that I would find a husband. I was bothered by the fact that she specified "husband" and wished for a world where my family could just accept me and the relationship I chose as is. The distance I felt with my family continued to grow.

Not long after, I found a new job with better pay. She and I made the big decision to move into an apartment together. We decided on a two-bedroom apartment, though we stayed in the same room together. Something about having the second bedroom gave me relief about the possible questions we could be asked at our new jobs or from family and friends who still didn't know about us. Somehow, it made me feel more honest, though in hindsight, I realize it was quite the opposite.

We had such a fun time living on our own and continuing to do everything together. The difference was that we weren't living with anyone else, so we were really able to maximize our time together. When she found a job she was quick to come out to her coworkers. I, however, did not. I kept my life at home private and referred to her as my roommate. I didn't want to feel the permanency I felt in telling my parents with people I had just met.

Our apartment happened to be across the street from a church. Driving past the church partially intimidated me and partially excited me. We were well over two years into our relationship, and somewhere amidst our time together, I realized that I couldn't grow in my relationship with her and God at the same time. I so badly wanted the two to work together, but every time I tried to reconcile them, I came up with a loss. I thought maybe attending a church together could be the answer. I was thrilled when she agreed we should check the church out. Over the next year, we went to the church a couple of times, and every time I walked through the doors, I felt like I had a sign on me that said "LOST." I did my best not to make eye contact with members and made no real efforts to meet anyone besides a casual hello. The sanctuary was dark, and the music was loud, so it was easy to stay hidden in the crowd. It felt good to be back at church, and my biggest hope was to find confirmation in my relationship with her. I was hoping there would be a message that would permit us to continue living as we were. I hoped to receive a sign from the pastor or congregants that we were not living in sin. I wanted validation from Christians that our love for each other was not forbidden. I wanted God but what I wanted more was for God to allow me to be as I was.

No God or Know God

When I think back on my relationship with another woman, from the outside looking in, it appears to have come out of nowhere. Never having experienced a romantic attraction to another woman would make it seem like I just switched teams on a whim because what she had to offer was better than what I was used to. Sin does that sometimes. Something we never expected to take over our lives seemingly comes out of left field. In a moment we may not even recognize as weakness, we are offered something that looks too good to pass up. We fool ourselves into seeing the offer as an opportunity when, in reality, it is a temptation ready to take us in the opposite direction of God's will. When we live our lives in a self-centered way rather than a God-centered way, we ignore the fact that this type of "opportunity" is in opposition to God's goodness. We do not do our due diligence to go to God. Instead, we choose our carnal desires that lead us to a cascade of decisions ready to drown us. You see, it's out of the habit of listening to our feelings that is a gateway to that path of destruction. It's the habit of letting our desires dictate our choices instead of using discernment.

The pattern of choosing our own desires over God's will is not unique to us. Trading God's will for our plans has been occurring since the beginning of humanity. Like Esau, we lose sight of the value God has placed on our lives, and we trade His good eternal plan for temporary satisfaction (Genesis 25 NKJV). My decision to enter into a relationship with another woman, although it appears out of character in many ways, was not the only time I have traded God's will for my own. Before her, I had habitually listened to my feelings more often than God's truth. The pendulum of my day-to-day decisions consistently leaned towards my own longings. My decision to date her really wasn't all that shocking when you view my track record of seeking my will above all else.

Every day, we are faced with a multitude of decisions; however, the number can actually be narrowed down to two. Each decision is a reflection of the two choices we have in life - the goodness of heaven or the wickedness of hell. Every choice is *rooted* in either good or evil. Consequently, each choice *results* in either eternal good or evil. The most well-known verse in the Bible, John 3:16, puts it simply for us, "whoever believes in Him shall not perish but have eternal life." In our choice, there is no middle ground to how we live. *We can either know God or say no to God.* We become servants of God or remain slaves to our sinful nature. Every decision we make reflects who or what we choose to serve at any given moment. This sounds like a load of pressure to behave perfectly, and oftentimes, we are guilty of poor attempts to be perfect without the Perfector. Our efforts on our own are missed opportunities to see the power of God working in us. We often misinterpret what it means to follow God, hindering our ability to truly know Him. But it makes sense how we can misunderstand what following God means when we misunderstand who God is. Because of common misconceptions about Christianity, it's imperative we discover the nature of God and experience the purpose of His word.

There's a misconception *outside* the church that Christians are manipulated to follow the standards God has set in place. People often view Christians as a group of blinded people being controlled by a heartless, arrogant, and totalitarian god. In this way, Christians are seen as being coerced into obedience to often unnecessary regulations by a ruthless being. Skeptics tend to see the Bible as a set of unfair rules humans are bound to fail at following. For that reason, many people won't even consider looking into the Christian faith. Another misconception is commonplace *within* the church. Many Christian churchgoers have a misunderstanding of grace and believe our free will is an allowance for us to behave as we wish because God will always welcome us back. This view of God makes Him seem soft and subservient to our desire to disregard His standards and do as we please. Neither perspective paints a true picture of the gravity of our choice to follow God's plan or not.

Understanding who God is comes to us in two ways—reading the Bible and experiencing Him in our lives. At times, we rely too much on personal experience to understand God. When we merely rely on what happens in our personal lives, we are missing out on the entirety of the purpose God set in motion when He created the World. Putting too much emphasis on personal experience even causes us to read the Bible through our own perspective. We handpick scripture to suit our need for validation, encouragement, and a general feeling of God working things out for our personal gain. We look for ourselves instead of God. Though the Bible is filled with hope and promise for a new day, we limit its meaning to pertain to our life now. In reality, God's plan is far greater than any individual timestamp we have set our eyes on. The Bible is the story of God. It's a tangible source of discovering His character and plan. It's the history of who God has always been and evidence of who He will always be. The Bible isn't just a historical book. It is living just as scripture describes. "For the word of God is living and active, sharper than any two-edged sword, piercing to the division of soul and of spirit, of joints and of marrow, and discerning the thoughts and intentions of the heart" (Hebrews 4:12 ESV). It is the living Word of God that moves us and changes us. Without Biblical influence, we miss out on the fullness of who God is and who we are called to be.

When there is balance in our relationship with God between personal experience and through reading the Word, we encounter something beautiful. We receive an astounding revelation of God in real time that matches what He has revealed about Himself to humanity since the beginning of time. Like any relationship, growth in relationship with God takes time and effort. I'll be the first to admit that far too many times, I've sacrificed growing in my relationship with God for anything else that is tangible. I know I'm not alone in that. We tend to spend time with what's in front of us most, so if we aren't in the habit of picking up our Bible or taking time to pray, we will grab our phone to scroll through social media or turn on Netflix to catch up on the latest episode of our favorite show. We crave connection, and when we aren't connecting with God, we will connect with anyone or anything else that captures our attention. Sometimes, we connect with things we consider healthy and appear risk-free: the gym, reading, friends, and family. Other times, we connect with things that are clearly unhealthy: pornography, alcohol, or gambling. In reality, all things are risky and unhealthy if we allow them to take the throne of our lives. The throne belongs to God, and when we let anything else take His place, we miss out on the greatest connection we have available to us.

God deeply desires a relationship with us. He knows He is the only one who can truly fulfill the connection we desperately crave and constantly seek elsewhere. He is willing and ready to receive our love and affection just as much as He is willing and ready to reveal His perfect love and affection to us. A relationship with God is the only thing that will truly fulfill our deepest needs. Had I turned to God instead of entering into and continuing a romantic relationship with my female friend, I would have experienced His perfect love in a way I never could have imagined. If I had turned from that temptation and turned to God, I would have known Him in a deeper way than I had before. My decision to say no to God impaired my ability to know Him in that season. Thank the Lord, the story didn't stop there.

Never Too Late

God, the Almighty Creator of the Universe, who knows all and sees all things, doesn't leave us in our depravity unless we choose to stay there. His creation of us was done with the intention of unifying us to Him. That has been His plan all along. When sin entered the World, God began His work to bring humanity back to a right and holy standing with Him. His invitation for us to live as image-bearers is truly profound, considering all the ways we turn against Him. Far too often, we allow the temptations of our flesh to blind us from the glory of God. God is patient and kind. He allows us the opportunity to experience life as we see fit. Despite our choices, He continues to move and extends unmatched mercy when we return to Him.

There will be people who don't understand the gravity of the gospel. A heart that is willing, often described by Christians as "softened," will be open to hearing the truth of God's Word. An unveiling of truth is theirs for the taking. Jesus, speaking about the light of truth, said, "If anyone has ears to hear, let him hear...Take heed what you hear. With the same measure you use, it will be measured to you; and to you who hear, more will be given. For whoever has, to him more will be given; but whoever does not have, even what he has will be taken away from him" (Mark 4:23-25 NKJV). The more willing we are to hear and follow God's truth, the more we will see the work of God in us, through us, and around us. Whatever we will, meaning whatever we are most eager about, is a reflection of not only where our heart is but what we spend our time thinking about. When we are constantly thinking with skepticism or aiming to prove a point without a willingness to be wrong, we are bound to have an immovable heart and a mind that is unwilling to change.

The Bible tells us that hearts will be hard and unable to grasp the greatness of God's love for us (Ephesians 4:18). Those who haven't put their faith in God will not understand the magnitude of what it means to be considered image-bearers. To all who don't know the true God, the faith and the sacrifice we are called to will look foolish. We see it all throughout scripture. Isaiah prophesied hearts would be calloused, eyes closed, and ears dull (Isaiah 6:10 ESV). Jesus referenced this prophecy 700 years later when explaining why He speaks in parables. "Though seeing, they do not see; though hearing, they do not hear or understand. In them is fulfilled the prophecy of Isaiah" (Matthew 13:13-15 ESV). Several years later, Paul again reiterated the fact that hearts will be hard (Acts 28:26-27 ESV). Though Isaiah, Jesus, and Paul were each addressing issues that were occurring in Biblical times, the truth of today is the same. People will inevitably be unable to see God for who He is because of their calloused hearts.

Just as the Bible tells us that some will not be able to comprehend the truth of God's Word, we see that an open heart to God's call is a great place to begin growing a relationship with God. We can be confident that He is seeking a relationship with us. "Behold, I stand at the door and knock. If anyone hears my voice and opens the door, I will come in to him and eat with him, and he with me" (Revelation 3:20 ESV). When we come near to God, He will come near to us (James

4:8 ESV). We can have confidence that God loves those who love Him, and those who seek Him will find Him (Proverbs 8:17).

This happens the first time we are called to faith, and we may have a similar experience if we wander from God. Like the story of the prodigal son, God's love for us expands our failures. He celebrates our return to Him (Luke 15:11-32). Our pride or stubbornness often keep us from repenting and returning to God. We see clues that He is calling out to us but ignore it because we happen to really like the thing that took us away from God in the first place. We avoid admitting we are in the wrong because what we are doing "feels right." We justify again and again. And even so, God continues to move.

I remember a time in particular when I especially struggled with wanting to have both my relationship with my girlfriend and with God. I concluded that I couldn't have both. With that conclusion, I believed the lie that Satan wanted me to believe – that God was so disappointed in me that He probably didn't want me any longer. I knew I had turned my back on Him and assumed I was too far gone. Despite tangible reminders of His unconditional love, like Billboards reading "Jesus Loves You" and bumper stickers saying "Jesus saves," I believed my soul was irrecoverable.

How often do we get stuck in sin and think there is no way out? Or if there is a way out, the distance appears too great to get back to a right standing with God? How many times do we tell ourselves it's too late because we have already made our decision? How many reminders do we ignore that God is still ever so close and waiting with arms open for our return?

The reality is that our sin *should* keep us from God and *does* keep us from God *if and only if* we refuse to accept that Jesus closed the gap when He died for our sins. The second we stand in repentance and acknowledge that we need Jesus, our hearts become open to God's transformative ways. The veil of our pride and stubbornness lifts, and we begin to see the beauty of walking in line with God again.

Whether new to faith, spiritually immature, or returning to faith, the wonders of God will take time to learn. Only by Christ will the veil be lifted (2 Corinthians 3:14). Over time, in relationship with God we begin to see Him in a deeper and more meaningful way. As we grow closer to God, we begin to resonate with that which didn't make sense before. As we release our lives to God for His use, we begin to see just how grand His plan is with us in mind. His purpose becomes all-encompassing, and we get to see the part He desires for us to participate in. The closer we get to God, the clearer our identity in Him becomes. With clarity of our identity, freedom reigns.

> Now the Lord is the Spirit, and where the Spirit of the Lord is, there is freedom. And we all, who with unveiled faces contemplate the Lord's glory, are being transformed into his image with ever-increasing glory, which comes from the Lord, who is the Spirit.
>
> — 2 Corinthians 3:17-18

Chapter 9

Tree Stumps

I never found the Christian validation of my relationship with her that I had been hoping for. I didn't face direct opposition from people in the church (besides my parents), but again, those who knew about our relationship were quite limited to a select group of people. After we renewed our apartment lease for another year, we decided to attend the church across the street once more.

Entering the sanctuary was the same as the few times we had attended before: dark, loud, and easy to hide. The difference this time was me.

Overall, I didn't *feel* different, but in the weeks leading up to this service, there was a shift in what I wanted out of life. I wanted more than what I was experiencing and wasn't certain my path was leading me there.

I missed God.

I didn't want to admit it because my life was good. I was happy in general and had everything I wanted except God. It had been such a long time since I had talked to Him and even longer since I felt like I heard Him.

I was not expecting much by attending another service. I assumed it would be like the times before- feeling like I was checking my quarterly attendance box off. The worship music was good. It was upbeat and moving. The feeling I felt listening to it was familiar to what I had felt during worship before her. My heart was being tugged in a way it hadn't felt since then. Although the worship was stirring something in me, it wasn't until the sermon that I knew I was meant to be at that very service.

As the pastor introduced his message, the backdrop photo behind him was like a giant neon light blinking: "THIS MESSAGE IS FOR YOU." It was as if God had hand-picked the image just for me that day. Displayed was a larger-than-life photo of a tree stump covered in moss. I was immediately taken back to the decaying tree stump in the woods from years before.

Just as I had before, I felt the prompting of the Holy Spirit...*There is life in death.*

This message *was* for me. I couldn't tell you what any of the previous sermons were about from the past services we had been to. Truthfully, it had been years since I actually paid attention to a sermon. On this day, I didn't want to miss a thing.

I was on the edge of my seat as the pastor spoke about Samson's story. It was a story I had heard before but didn't remember much of. He preached about the faults of Samson. He used the example of Samson falling in love with Delilah, being manipulated and deceived by her, and then losing his God-given strength when she used his weakness against him. When the pastor spoke about weakness, mine became evident to me. I saw how the relationship I was in had diminished my God-given strengths. I didn't feel like a victim of my decisions. I felt the conviction of the Holy Spirit. The pastor wrapped up the message by sharing how God still used Samson despite his faults and did His greatest work through Samson in his death.

Samson was by no means the perfect example of a faithful Christian, but there is no denying that God used him in a remarkable way. I began to feel my heart pounding in my chest.

Could God still use me? Did God still want to use me?

As the pastor began to close the service in prayer, he said something that haunted me in the best way possible. It solidified what I already knew to be true about this message. It was the last piece of evidence that I was meant to hear this sermon at this particular time.

"There is a young woman here trying to shortcut her life, and God wants you to know you don't need to shortcut any longer."

I'm pretty certain I stopped breathing for a minute. There was no way I could brush off anything I had heard from the previous hour. God was speaking. The tears began to flow from my eyes. I felt God telling me it was time to come home. It was time to leave the life I was living behind. It was time to break up with my girlfriend.

As the tears streamed down my face, I could feel her eyes on me. She leaned over and asked if everything was ok. Immediately, I went into flight mode and thought of how I could justify my tears. I didn't want to do what God was asking me to do. At the same time, I could no longer ignore His prompts. He spoke so clearly to me in that sanctuary that I knew rejecting His prompting would be the biggest mistake of my life.

He was asking for my obedience in cutting off the relationship.

I had never been so nervous as she and I walked silently to the car. The years we spent together flashed before my eyes. The worry of losing her became overwhelming. We sat in the car for what felt like an eternity, but was more accurately, only minutes. She asked what was wrong. I couldn't look her in the eyes as I told her what I had just experienced. I tried to talk my way around the topic of breaking up but eventually, it was decided...we were breaking up.

I wish I could tell you that that was the end of everything. I wish I could say, I packed my things, I moved out, we both moved on, and I continued growing in my faith. Unfortunately, I continued to get in the way of God. I justified continuing to live with her because I didn't want to break the lease, and selfishly, I didn't want to lose her in my life as a friend. I did a terrible job at setting and practicing boundaries. Though we had a two-bedroom apartment, and I could have at least moved permanently into my own room, I continued to share a room with her more often than not. I wasn't willing to give up the comfort of being next to her in order to step into what God was calling me to.

The next year of our lease exemplified my lack of full obedience to God. I knew He was calling me to let go of the relationship completely, but I continued to give in to my fleshly desires of love and acceptance. I lacked trust that God would provide friends and community for me if I fully left her, and my selfishness only made things harder in the end.

Chopped Down

As we've discussed previously, the Holy Spirit is at work in believers and in the church to prune branches that are not bearing fruit. Sometimes, a much more drastic approach must happen in our lives to move forward toward God's will. In my experience, turning my back on God for four-plus years led me to need quite an overhaul of my life. Although I had seemed happy from the outside looking in and often tricked myself into believing I was still living (a mostly) Christian life, I was lying to myself.

I tried to abide by the worldly belief that my love for her wasn't harming anyone else. *All love is love, isn't it?*

I tried to fit my sin and selfishness into Christianity. Anything during those years that appeared to be a fruit of the Spirit was merely me being a *good person* rather than a *Godly person*.

The love I gave came with conditions of others accepting me and my decisions.

The joy I exuded wasn't joy but rather happiness.

Peace I brought was merely to avoid confrontation.

My kindness served as a side to discrete selfish ambitions.

My patience was under the pretense of doing things my way and in my time.

Goodness was not true goodness because it was transactional.

My faithfulness was for her when it should have been for God.

I may have been gentle in my words but I was not gentle in thought.

Self-control was situational because clearly I lacked self-control in my own desires.

The characteristics I displayed came from my own volition and for my own good feelings. I wanted to be known as a nice person but didn't care about the eternal impact the rest of my life was having on those around me.

The fruits in my life had rotted. The branches were full of disease, if not fully dead. Without a doubt, the entire tree needed to be cut down.

Here's the thing - when God asks us to cut down something in our life, He is calling us to repentance. He is calling us to turn from sin and to return to Him. This can sound like a lot when you're in deep, I know...

Like the parable of the barren fig tree, when we are bearing no fruit, God is patient with us. He gives time for the redemptive power of Christ to work in us. As much as He is patient, He is just. If we do not choose repentance, we face His holy wrath (Luke 13:6-9 ESV). The heaviness of this statement is not meant to cause us to worry; it is meant to keep us attentive with our eyes set on things above (Colossians 3:2 ESV). It is meant to encourage us to keep our hearts open to God's will.

God Decides and God delivers

God decides what is good and what needs to be removed. He will reveal to us what is holding us back from His will. He knows cutting down sin in our lives is difficult and even painful. He is compassionate and wants nothing more than to walk us through the pain to show us His glory.

Jehovah Mephalti, The Lord my Deliverer, plans beauty out of our pain.

He wants to take us from where we've been stuck into a place of freedom. All it takes is an open heart for our ears to hear (Matthew 13:15 ESV). In our willingness, God promises to deliver us from our rebellious ways into something marvelous.

It's hard to see the beauty to come when we are in the midst of pain. Like Job in his pessimism:

> For there is hope for a tree, if it be cut down, that it will sprout again, and that its shoots will not cease. Though its root grow old in the earth, and its stump die in the soil, yet at the scent of water it will bud and put out branches like a young plant...But a man dies and is laid low; he breathes his last and is no more.

Tiffany Sullivan

—Job 14:7-9, 10 NKJV

Job saw that a tree cut down has the potential for new life but despaired about the finality of mankind's death. Though Job appears to be speaking literally, we can take a lesson from his hopelessness. We tend to lose hope that God will turn our ashes into beauty. At times we question our eternity. We even give others the benefit of the doubt when it comes to their testimony. We see God working through their sin and pain...but ours?

As if there's disparity in our own testimony of God's goodness, we believe we will be left alone in our suffering. We decide we are too unworthy of mercy and struggle to see the grace of new growth that God plants in us.

In Job's anguish-filled questions, we see glimpses of the truth that was planted in his heart: "I will wait till my change comes" (Job 14:14 NKJV). An important lesson we can learn from Job is that in his pessimism and through his questions, there was a bud of hope. In our own wrestlings between hope and despair, our best bet is to cling to whatever glimmer of hope we see.

We've seen He's been good before, so what's stopping Him now?

We've read the testimonies of how God shows up. Why wouldn't He do the same for us?

And even if our faith is still fragile, God is still moving. Though Job had weak and wavering hope throughout his suffering, the Lord was faithful. God does the same for us. He promises to strengthen us when we eagerly wait for the change to come (Isaiah 40:29-31 ESV).

Once we've experienced any sort of cutting down, new growth takes time. God is so kind to tend to us when we are in the vulnerable and raw place of leaving behind what we once knew. He is patient to show us His way as we adjust to giving up our way. His timing is perfect. His approach is perfect. Like a gardener, He knows the amount of water and sunlight needed and when they are needed. He doesn't flood us with right and wrong but showers us with holy love. He doesn't scorch us with unfair judgment, but in righteousness covers us with mercy.

The sermon He used to pull me out of my relationship with another woman wasn't a sermon full of brimstone and fire. He didn't use a blatant message about homosexuality being the pathway to hell but gave me a clear indication that what I was walking in was keeping me from Him. He knew that I had been questioning my salvation throughout those years. He knew my heart needed a real answer; *He was always and will always be the answer.* He saw the yearning of my heart to experience true love and revealed Himself as the One I needed all along. In my wavering year preceding the break-up, He never left me. I had new hope in Him but despaired greatly in my loss. Through the complications that I created during that time, He continued to call me into His faithfulness.

I share this to offer hope in the truth that God hasn't left you and will never leave you. He knows what your heart needs.

The Remnant

Remains of our past are inevitable. Even if only memories, these remains - the remnant - are evidence of what we lived through and the lessons we've learned. It isn't abnormal for the remains of our circumstances to look like bitterness, triggers, guilt, or grief. The weight of the remains can feel just as heavy as the trial...

God wants to lighten the load of the remnant. He offers us a different perspective. He wants the trials and tribulations we experience to bring us closer to Him, and there, He promises to reveal something new (Isaiah 43:19 ESV).

He wants to transform our memories of what once was bitter, triggering, guilt-ridden, or grief-stricken into the peace that His freedom inexplicably brings. He wants our memories and what He has done through them to be what evokes us to remain steadfast in Him. He knows that holding onto the things of the past is dangerous and desires us to release our burdens to Him. As believers, when we cast our cares on the Lord, the Bible tells us that He will sustain us and keep us steady (Psalm 55:22 ESV).

I picture this promise much like a tree stump covered in moss...the roots anchor the remaining bit of the tree in solid ground...the vibrant moss; new life, all around...Most of the tree needed removing, yet so much beauty is found in the loss.

Whether cut down or dead from disease, a tree stump, is what is left after the tree falls. The remnant of the tree, a trace left behind, marking the sturdiness of what lies below and the unsteadiness of what once stood atop.

"Remnant" is used throughout the Bible 540 times to describe the remaining groups of people who survived or escaped destruction.[1] Remnants of people were often salvaged by and for God after His acts of judgment. These people were a trace of truth and loyalty set apart for a holy purpose, with God's promises weaved throughout their stories.

A promise of restoration: In the day of Noah, when the earth was overrun by sinfulness, God had to do something drastic. He put an end to the sinful destruction that had taken over and set Noah and his family apart as the remnant of the restoration of life on earth. He sent the greatest flood of all time to reclaim His purpose for the World (Genesis 6:17-18 ESV).

A promise of freedom: Joseph, full of God's grace, reunited with his brothers, who sold him into slavery leading him to years of suffering. He realized the purpose of his suffering as preparation for a remnant marked by liberation; "But God sent me ahead of you to preserve for you a remnant on earth and to save your lives by a great deliverance" (Genesis 45:7).

A promise of connectedness: God tells Elijah, who wondered if he was the last faithful servant remaining, that He reserved a remnant of 7,000 Israelites who had not bowed down to Baal. He reminded Elijah of the community of believers who remained with him (1 Kings 19:18).

Over and over again, groups of people were pulled away from destruction and set apart for God's purpose. Though the destruction was necessary for God's judgment to rid areas of the sin that was running rampant, God's mercy remained. In His mercy, God saved a portion in order to resume His restoration of righteousness.

The concept of the remnant wasn't just for Old Testament times. Stories throughout the Bible of those remaining after destruction represent that God continues to hold to His promises today. The nature of God's reparative ways in the midst of wickedness stands as a testimony of who God is.

He is the God who uses the residue for restoration.

He is the God who offers freedom from our failures.

He is the God who, when we feel the loss, provides comfort through our connection to Him.

The remnants in our lives have purpose. God's plan for the remains is astonishing. The way He chooses to build us back up after we've walked so far from Him is astounding. God is the Master of renovation. The right to restoration is ours through Christ. When we regard God's warnings and choose repentance, we are marked by faithfulness. We are grafted in like the remnant God uses for His redemptive plan for the World (Romans 11:22-24 ESV).

Hearing God's promises doesn't always make it easier to trust Him...

Sometimes, we cling to what's left over from our past in fear of what could happen with full surrender. We feel safer hanging on to whatever control we can in the midst of so much loss. Our decision to avoid fully releasing it all to God keeps us from the entire picture of what He desires in our lives.

During the year I remained living with my ex-girlfriend, I clung to comfort. I didn't want to experience the heartache of losing her completely in my life, so I lived in partial obedience. The tug-of-war I felt between my flesh and my spirit was constant. I became a fence-sitter in my convictions. It was rather uncomfortable, but I was too afraid of what full surrender would look like. I wasn't allowing God to carry the burden of my past and I surely wasn't trusting Him fully with my future. Instead, I was still trying to navigate this new life on my own.

We have a tendency to do that in faith. We want the outcome but still want to do things our way. It's essentially a have my cake and eat it too moment. We would rather choose what we hold onto and what we let go of because full surrender is filled with uncertainty. The reality is that God allows us that choice. He never forces us to surrender into full obedience. The caveat is that when we do not fully obey, we are left to deal with the consequences.

Partial obedience puts us at high risk of back-sliding. The danger of returning to old ways can actually leave us worse off than we were in the first place because we know better exists. The Bible instructs us, in our holy purpose, not to comply with our previous ignorance (1 Peter 1:14 ESV). So, once we are aware of what God is calling us to surrender, it's our responsibility to run away from our weaknesses by running to the Spirit of Christ who frees us.

The Holy Seed

We are inadequate on our own to make good, eternal purpose out of our pain, our sin, and our weaknesses. No amount of striving for and doing better can make up for the fact that there is an eternal purpose we are incapable of achieving by our own will.

We need redemption. What we've faced needs redemption.

We are in a world afflicted by sin that's in the process of being saved. It's difficult to see redeeming hope when we are constantly faced with the consequences of sin. It feels impossible to anticipate the glory to come when we are in the middle of suffering. Words of encouragement seem unproductive when we are witness to others' agony. And in the times that seem so hopeless, our need for a Savior is ever-so-evident. Thank God for His written Word...

The Old Testament continuously points to the need and fulfillment of salvation. The stories are wild displays of wickedness in the World. The destruction of cities and people who refused to follow God stand as warnings of what will happen if we continue to live apart from Him. The chaotic history of the Old Testament isn't merely a warning—it shows us the hope we have.

Isaiah, a book full of warnings and prophecies of hope, tells the story of a holy seed coming out of the remnant of Judah..."*like a terebinth or an oak, whose stump remains when it is felled. The holy seed is its stump*" (Isaiah 6:13 ESV). By this holy seed was the promise of the Redeemer, the One True God who made all things

(Isaiah 44:6 & 24). Whether Isaiah was referring to Christ or His bloodline as the seed, his prophecy came to fruition when Jesus was born, lived a perfect death, and died for the atonement of our sins. He is the one who saves us from the death we deserve. Redemption from death to life, which the World so desperately needs, is in Christ (Ephesians 1:7). Like moss on a tree stump, Jesus is a holy seed that became a tangible example of life in death.

Besides the undeserving salvation we are offered through Christ's death, the holy seed implies hope for our daily lives. Jesus isn't just the moss that covers the tree stump. Like a shoot growing from a stump, Christ is the one whom, when planted in us, true life grows out of. He is the source that brings forth fruit in our lives (Isaiah 11:1 ESV). Without His life and death on the cross, no resurrection would exist. Without the resurrection, we would be void of the powerful workings of the Holy Spirit in our lives. This was *always* God's redemptive plan. It doesn't matter how far we've walked away from God. In us, by the power of the Holy Spirit, there will be fruit that confirms Christ in our lives.

And by the fruit, we will experience our own life in death.

The fruit from a seed often emerges by unassuming growth. Something that appears so tiny, a seed, has an immense capability to grow into something unimaginably great and beautiful. At first appearance, a seed may not look to have such great power, but over time, as the seed is planted and watered, we begin to see what grows from it.

The same can be said about our walk with Christ. Initially, we won't see the full picture of what He plans to do in us and through us. But over time, as our relationship continues to grow and we experience the presence of the Holy Spirit more, we get to see fruits spring to life. The amazing thing about the growth we experience is how natural and unforced it is when it's genuinely coming from the life-giving source of the holy seed of Jesus Christ.

If you can't tell by now, I have quite an affinity for the botanical imagery the Bible uses to represent our spiritual growth. I find the resemblance to be profound... Plants are grown physically by a replication of DNA. Similarly, we grow spiritually in our imitation of Christ. Much like a plant, our growth is organic, with a need for nurturing and tending to see the final fruits. Our spiritual growth is subtle at a glimpse yet seen suddenly in time, like the flowering of a plant. One day, seemingly out of nowhere, a flower appears atop the stem that has been in preparation for the flowering for some time. Likewise, God is at work in us, oftentimes unnoticeably, and one day, the fruit of His presence becomes noticeable.

The seasons of growth in plants are parallel to our seasons of growth in Christ. We experience summer- when everything appears bright and colorful. When we enter fall, life begins to look different - dry, and the colors begin to fade. In winter, everything seems to be dead, yet under the surface of the soil, the roots are receiving much-needed nutrients. Then in spring, new life shoots up without much notice.[2] The various seasons of our life are necessary for growth, just as the seasons in nature are needed for plants to thrive. Regardless of how much growth we experience here and now, the holy seed of Christ gives us eternal purpose in all things.

Thankful for the Thorns

It's no secret that none of us want to experience pain in life. We don't ask for the struggles we face, yet for some reason, hardship is often the catalyst required to meet Christ more intimately. At times in our sin and suffering, we get to see the good that comes from it. We see God in it. The silver lining is a sweet reminder of grace and mercy. Other times we are left to wonder what good could ever come from such terrible circumstances. We wonder how God could possibly be with us in those moments. Begging to understand, we don't see the good on this side of heaven. I can't offer much more than empathy and compassion for the latter. I have my own questions. What is offered to us all though is assurance. Like the rose that blooms amidst a bush full of thorns, we are given the gift of confidence in God's perfect plan out of the brokenness of this world. We might not be there to see the rose, but we know for certainty it's going to bloom. God's Word gives us similar expressions of hope:

Flawlessness is ours. Our fleshly nature, though full of flaws, is considered unblemished. Though we are still being made holy, God already sees the perfection to come in eternity (Hebrew 10:14).

Our pain will be reclaimed. God is the God of making possible what was once impossible. We have the opportunity to see beauty from ashes, gladness instead of mourning, and praise instead of despair (Isaiah 61:3-4).

Everything will be used with intention. Our suffering is not wasted- not even an ounce of it. God has called us to Him, and with that comes the reassurance that all things will work out for His good purpose (Romans 8:28).

Restoration will come. No matter how weak we feel or how little value we see in our circumstances, God's way supersedes. God of all grace promises to restore, strengthen, confirm and establish us (1 Peter 5:10).

Coming Out Restored

We will see unmatchable glory. Our current circumstances will be outweighed by what is coming on the other side of heaven. The suffering we experience now won't come close to the glory to be revealed (Romans 8:18).

From Genesis to Revelation, we see the certainty that God offers. We read His promises from the beginning and see them being uncovered throughout the history of the Bible. Since the genesis of the world, evil has been intended for good (Genesis 50:20). Until the end when the full promise is revealed, all things are being made new (Revelation 21:5). When God calls us to Him, we feel the weight of our burdens begin to lift. We see our problems a little bit differently. We get glimpses of His glory here on Earth. As we walk with Him, our capability of gratitude shifts from what we currently see to what will come. We begin to see purpose in the hard parts of life and in time we realize the presence of the thorn makes the rose that much more beautiful.

Chapter 10

Seeing Sunflowers

As our lease neared its end, the reality of not knowing what was next began to sink in. I knew that something different needed to happen in order for God's plan to come to fruition. I knew the closeness I maintained with my ex-girlfriend was holding me back from moving forward. I was still toeing the line of inappropriate boundaries in my attempts to keep the friendship. We looked at new apartments together, and I found one I really loved. Sitting in the leasing office discussing costs and facing the reality that the budget would only afford a one-bedroom apartment, I realized I was still desperate to have my way. I knew I would be making a massive mistake continuing to live with her, so I did the only thing I knew at the time. I started planning my escape from Florida. I wasn't sure if I would move to Iowa temporarily to live with my grandma or really suck up my pride and move back home to live with my parents until I figured out what to do next. All I knew at the time was that staying was a bad idea because I wasn't trustworthy on my own.

I began to sell everything I could on Facebook Marketplace.

As items were purchased and picked up, the unknown of my future seemed more and more bleak. A part of me was concerned for the future, while the other part of me felt relief knowing we would not be moving in together again. I continued hoping to keep the friendship going despite not knowing what it would look like. I still couldn't imagine life completely void of the best friend I had known for five years. One day I received a message from a guy on Facebook Marketplace regarding a guitar I had up for sale. The guitar had already been purchased, and I informed him that if he was looking for anything else, I had plenty of other items up for grabs. I was surprised when he messaged back, saying he may actually be interested in a chair I had for sale. I looked at his profile like I did with all potential buyers to ensure he was a real person and seemed trustworthy. *He's sort of cute.* The thought caught me off guard because it had been years since I felt attracted to anyone else. I scrolled through his profile and realized he played on a worship team for church. My curiosity peaked. Cute, Christian, and male? My interest in knowing more was slightly alarming yet considerably comforting. I believed I was broken and hadn't even considered the option of being with a Christian man after breaking up with a female. I hadn't even begun to think about how I would handle a potential attraction to one. Well, I handled it the only way I knew how. I was overly eager to meet. I hadn't cared to look presentable for anyone else interested in buying anything but I made sure I got ready for him. I wasn't certain, but he seemed eager to meet me as well. It made me nervous but awakened something I hadn't felt in years.

When he came to look at my chair, I felt a spark. Although he kindly declined the chair, I could sense that maybe he had just used the chair as an excuse to meet me in person. I welcomed the thought. Within hours of meeting he messaged me, striking up a conversation. Within a few days of our first message, we were spending hours texting and talking on FaceTime. I officially moved into the spare bedroom so I could stay up at night talking to him. He had asked why I was selling everything, and when I broke the news that I had plans to move out of Florida, he expressed his disappointment. "I was hoping to take you out on a date." His comment felt like further validation that moving out and moving on was what God was calling me to. Within a couple of weeks, we went on a first date. I nervously told him about the last several years, and though he seemed a little caught off guard, his interest in me was still there. He repeatedly asked me to stay in Tampa. I told him I didn't really have an option but to leave because I hadn't found an apartment yet. To my surprise, he said I could come live with him. He had a two-bedroom house and said the spare bedroom could be mine. Since we had been talking so much, he didn't feel like the stranger he was. I agreed to move in.

When I broke the news to my ex-girlfriend, she felt betrayed, to say the least. My change in attitude towards her was obvious. She didn't understand how I could move on so quickly and said I appeared cold to her. My excitement about him made it easier to accept my responsibility in the hurt I was causing her without feeling a need to smooth things over with her. My affections had changed. I believed God had ordained this new relationship. As callous as it sounds, leaving her was easy at that point. I had known for over a year that God was calling me away, and it seemed like He was throwing me one last line to reel me out of the hole I had dug myself into. This guy felt like some sort of redemption plan, and I was more than open to the idea.

Soon after, he and I made things official. I had a boyfriend. After years of believing I would live the rest of my life with a woman, I had a boyfriend. A Christian boyfriend at that.

Immediately, my heart was set on marrying this guy. According to him, that's what he had in mind as well. He admitted to me that when we first met, he felt like God was directing him to invite me to move into his place. It felt like another confirmation I was where God wanted me. I was beyond grateful. My new relationship seemed to be pointing me toward God in a way I hadn't experienced previously. He had a stack of Christian books, and I began reading one after another. He had suggestions for different sermon series that I immersed myself in. I began to feel like I was healing from the self-inflicted emotional wounds I had caused the previous several years. I felt the presence of God more. I heard from God more. In the wind. On the waves. By the trees. God felt so near.

As quickly as our relationship grew, it withered at the same pace. My birthday was about a month and a half after I moved into his house. My parents decided to make a trip to Florida, and I was thrilled to introduce them to each other. The meeting seemed awkward, but I assumed it was because I was living with him, and although they wouldn't say it, they didn't think it was the best idea. We all stayed at the beach for a night, and he seemed to want to do his own thing. He said he thought I should just enjoy time with my parents and that he didn't want to intrude. I did my best to reassure him but could tell something was off. After my parents left, things continued to feel less than ideal, but I remained hopeful. *Maybe he had cold feet and just needed a little space.*

I knew without a doubt something was wrong when his mom came to the house to drop something off, and he wouldn't let me go outside to meet her. He told me she didn't know he had a girlfriend. I was hurt but again tried to be understanding and let it go after I expressed my concern. I still believed God had ordained this relationship. Within a couple months however, it was clear that I was trying to hang on to something that wasn't there. He said he needed some space and it was obvious he meant it. He avoided being in common spaces when I was home. I felt un-welcomed but was still clinging to the hope that God had put us together. Instead of seeing the signs and deciding to move into my own place, I dug my heels in and stayed a little longer. I think he had hoped I would move out on my own but when he asked if I had been looking for places and I responded "no" he told me he thought it would be best. The rejection was crushing but I felt deserving of it.

I began to look for apartments and during that time, God gave me so much peace. I still had hope that things could work out but trusted God had a plan for me. I began to pray expectantly for both of us. Within those prayers, God shifted my focus toward Himself. I found an apartment and within a month I moved out on my own for the first time since I had lived in Florida. I felt so alone but strangely at peace. I missed the companionship I was accustomed to the past several years but felt comfort and a growing affection in my relationship with God.

I finally tried connecting at the church I had gone to a few times with my ex-girlfriend. I decided to join a Bible study. I was eager to meet new friends. As the first meeting approached, I found myself in anticipation of what the Lord was going to do in me through that Bible study. My hopes were high. The night of the Bible study, I was slightly nervous but still eager. I showed up a couple minutes early, so I thought. I knocked on the door and on the other side was a girl who looked quite surprised to see me. I thought maybe I had gone to the wrong apartment. She informed me I was at the right place but the wrong time. I was an hour early and she wasn't quite prepared for company yet. I told her it was fine and I would be back in an hour. The encounter was discouraging and I thought about not returning but felt the Lord prompting me to return. I became excited again with anticipation for what would happen that night. I had hopes of good Biblical discussion with a group of God-fearing women who would become close friends of mine.

Well the Lord humbled my plans when I returned an hour later to find out I was the only one attending the group that night. This was not what I was expecting, but God has a funny way of doing things sometimes. It felt like God was saying, "I'm going to give you relationships with others, but it's going to be at my pace and my way this time." We sat at her dining room table, and in the middle was a vase with a sunflower in it. For some reason, the sunflower especially stood out to me. We discussed the story of the alabaster jar in the Bible. It is about giving God our best and our all. Giving Him my all seemed rather easy at the moment because I had nothing else and no one else to give my attention or affection to. No significant other to distract me. No friends to distract me. God was giving me a clean slate to follow through in chasing what my heart truly wanted...Him.

As I settled into my new apartment, I felt like the church and Bible study may not be a good fit for me in that season. It was rather far from my apartment, and I still hadn't built a community there. I found myself looking into a church close to my current apartment that my most recent ex-boyfriend just so happened to have mentioned previously. On my first visit to the church, I felt like I was meant to make it my church home. Soon after I started going regularly, I joined a Bible study. I didn't know a single person, but the study was based on Lysa Tyrkeurst's book, "Uninvited." At the time I was really struggling with feeling rejected and felt hopeless in making girlfriends. I began to believe the lie that I was unworthy of a relationship with a Christian guy because of my past. I also began believing the lie that I would not be able to make friends with girls without them assuming I had feelings for them. I certainly felt uninvited and unwelcome in many ways, but God continued to remind me of His unconditional love for me. I felt His presence in the midst of my loneliness and knew in my heart that He had me where He wanted me.

Face the Son

Throughout months of living in solitude, God felt exceedingly present. I truly have never felt so close to Him in my life. Several times, I felt like I could actually feel His hand embracing mine, as I thanked Him for what He was doing and clung to Him in the unknown. My life was consumed with gratitude amidst the ruins left from letting go of doing things my way. I often found myself especially sad about the most recent breakup. Although our relationship was short-lived, I had a lot of hope for a future with him. After we broke up, the rejection stung for a while, but every time I felt the sting, I prayed aloud for him, for me, and for God's plan in each of our lives. I thanked God for the pain. I thanked God for the unknown. I thanked God because I knew that He was all I needed and I would never lose Him.

During those months of healing, I saw sunflowers everywhere and I mean everywhere. On billboards, on bumper stickers, on shirts, on dresses, on aprons, on the side of the road. I saw them everywhere and nearly everyday. I had a feeling God was trying to get my attention again. This time it felt less dooming. Every time I saw a sunflower, it was like a kiss from heaven and a reminder that God was near.

I went home to Colorado for a week and it happened to be sunflower season. I drove by miles and miles of sunflowers over the course of that trip. About halfway through I decided to stop on the side of the road and couldn't help myself in picking the perfect one. As I went to pull it from the ground, I realized just how sturdy their stems are. I had never picked a sunflower before. I had to bend and twist it in order to break it free and when I did, the break was not clean. The stem was quite stringy by the time I was through with it. As I sat in the car looking at my now less-than-perfect sunflower, I couldn't help but wonder what was so special about these flowers. I had never been drawn to sunflowers in the past. I also never thought they were very pretty, but man, the strength and sturdiness surely stood out in that moment. I went back to my parent's house and decided I should do a little research on the flowers. I was beside myself when I learned just how amazing these plants are.

 A single sunflower can produce 1,000 - 2,000 sunflower seeds. The sunflower seed is actually a fruit due to the fact that it is a seed-bearing structure that is formed after flowering. Each sunflower seed can be replanted to grow another flower that will produce the "fruit" again. The entirety of a sunflower is used for many purposes. Sunflowers produce one large central root called a "taproot" that grows a meter deep into the soil. Taproots are the primary source of nutrition and stability, anchoring them. Secondary roots remain close to the top of the soil and can spread out to a similar length of one meter. Due to the depth of the root system, sunflowers grow well in dry and sunny locations. Unlike many other flowers, they are capable of surviving in drought-like conditions and will still bloom under stressful conditions.[1] When the flower blooms, the root reaches maximum depth in the soil.

 Sunflowers are called sunflowers not only because they have a strikingly large round center and the surrounding petals resemble sunbeams. They are also called sunflowers because of their dependence on the sun. Their circadian rhythm or internal clock is aligned with the pattern of the sun throughout the day to achieve proper growth and development. As the earth rotates, young sunflowers with pliable stems turn to face the sun as it rises and sets, taking in as much light as possible. Heliotropism is the term that describes the behavior of the sunflower. The root word for the latter half, "tropos," means "a turn, change." As sunflowers mature and their stems become sturdy and inflexible, they stay facing the East to meet the sun as it rises and take in all of the benefits of the warmth of the morning sun.[2]

In my research on sunflowers, I realized we are so similar to them:

We are made to resemble the Son of God. In the way a sunflower resembles the sun, we are made in God's image and created to bear the likeness of His Son. As we grow in faith, we grow in our resemblance to Christ. The Bible says, "We are being transformed into His image" (2 Corinthians 3:18 ESV).

Keeping our eyes on Jesus provides the light we need to fulfill our purpose. Like the young and maturing sunflowers in their heliotropism, when we turn to face the Son, we receive the light we need in order to develop spiritually. Jesus is the light of the world (John 8:12 ESV). Our internal clock is wired to be in line with the Light of the World. It only makes sense when we are walking in His light; we are more equipped for and synchronized with the needs of those around us.

Fruits plant seeds. The fruit of the Holy Spirit that grows in us comes from the seed that's been planted in us. Our fruit is intended, in turn, to become seeds sown in the lives of those around us. There are thousands upon thousands of opportunities day in and day out to plant seeds. In fact, we are called to do so and are told we will reap what we sow (2 Corinthians 9:6 ESV).

The root sustains us. In our faithfulness to plant seeds, God remains faithful by causing the seeds to grow (1 Corinthians 3:6 ESV). In order to fulfill all the purposes we were made for, we must be anchored in the seed that is Christ (Hebrews 6:19 ESV). When our roots are firmly planted in truth, we are made to withstand the heat and dry seasons (Jeremiah 17:8 ESV).

Our spiritual growth helps us stand strong. As we become mature Christians, we are less pliable and less persuaded by the temptations of the World. Like the mature sunflower that faces the East to meet the sunrise we stand confident in and can bask in the truth of the risen Son without concern of what's behind us. We can trust that in our maturity, our lives will impact the world (Matthew 5:14-16 NKJV).

Intentional Design

Like the sunflower, we are created with so much significance and intention. Our creation as Imago Dei, the image of the almighty God, is central to our being. Imago Dei is at the core of who we are despite our brokenness and the sinful world we reside in. We cannot avoid the divine design God had in mind for us when He decided to breathe us into existence. Think about the gravity of being God-breathed. His holy and perfect breath gave us life. It is said by scholars and rabbis that His breath is even in our lungs. We speak His name every time we breathe. YHWH.

Inhale- "YH," exhale "WH."[3]

When He decided to breathe us into existence, perfection was His plan. His perfect purpose will come to pass. We long for that day. The deepest parts of us ache to live in the perfect image of Christ; the design we were made to be. Truly experiencing life with God comes with the realization that life without God feels void of the greatest love you've ever known. If you haven't truly experienced life with God, there's an inexplicable void you feel that you are bound to attempt to fill with something or someone. Oftentimes we hear it described as a "God-shaped hole" in our heart. Until we feel Him fill the void we don't realize it was Him all along we were missing. Without God, we chase the things of this world in hopes to fulfill what our hearts are missing. Money, success, and relationships are all used to fill the gaps in our deepest need - a relationship with Christ.

Finding true love in relationships is romanticized as an appropriate way to feel wholeness. "He/she completes me," "my better half," and "my soulmate" is ingrained in us as the goal of lifelong partnerships. We are taught at a young age that our aim in life is to get married and have children of our own. These aren't bad goals to have. Relationships are good. We were made for them. Without God though, they have no eternal value (1 Corinthians 7:31 ESV). Once we are in relationship with Christ, we experience the war between our imperfect human nature and the perfect design God had in mind. We don't become more comfortable in this world. In fact, we often feel less belonging here as our hearts ache for what's ahead. We yearn for that perfect design we were made to replicate (Romans 8:22-23 ESV). We can rest assured that the day of perfection is coming. He will recover us and reclaim us to the perfect design He started in the Garden of Eden. His intention will come to pass.

God's intentionality in design is evident all over Earth. Everything in creation was calculated with thought and meaning. To design is to create for a specific function or end. Design isn't just the make up of what is created. Design is about purpose. Our design isn't just *how we were made* but *why we were made*. Design points not merely what we were created as - tall, short, assertive, meek, male, female etc. Design points to why we were created as we were. God had intent when He made me as He did, just as He had intent with how He made you. Purpose and intention are at the core of who we are. And unless we are living our purpose out, we fail to function at our full potential. God is a God of purpose and intention in all things.

In my research of sunflowers, God revealed His intentional design in a way that typically does not resonate with me through math and science. Ordinarily, I would run for the hills if I was presented with anything beyond basic understanding in either topic. Despite my lack of understanding of such topics, God revealed to me that math and science are actually evidence of His intention in creation. If you also are not a science or math person, bear with me.

The Golden Ratio is a fascinating phenomenon seen all throughout creation that points to a very particular and purposeful design plan surrounding numbers. The ratio is both pleasing to the eye and plays a purpose in various plants, weather patterns, and even our own bodies. The Fibonacci Sequence is an order of numbers that helps us understand the Golden Ratio. The mathematical sequence is one in which the sum of the two preceding numbers equals the next number in the sequence. Starting with 0 and 1, the sequence looks like this:

$$0, 1, 1, 2, 3, 5, 8, 13, 21, 34, 55, 89, 144....$$

Not only do these numbers appear frequently in mathematics, but they appear in biology as well. Tree branches, pine cone bracts, and the arrangement of leaves on stems are a few examples. Likewise, the count of petals on different flowers like lilies and buttercups follows the Fibonacci Sequence. The Golden Ratio, considered to be a divine proportion, is the ratio between two numbers that equals approximately 1.618. The ratio of any two consecutive numbers from the Fibonacci sequence results in a number close to 1.618. The further up the sequence you go, the closer that number gets to that perfect ratio of 1.618. You can see this for yourself. For example, divide 144 by its preceding number in the Fibonacci sequence, 89, and you get the number 1.61797753.[4]

So how does this relate to sunflowers, and why does it matter? It comes back to God's intention in how He designed everything. For some reason, the Golden Ratio is seen all throughout creation. It isn't just seen in an aesthetically pleasing layout of the pattern of petals on flowers, fern leaves, and branch patterns. It shows up in the spiral of seashells, the pattern of hurricanes, and our very own DNA. Scientists have recently determined that the height of a DNA helix unit is equivalent to the Golden Ratio. That is, 34 angstroms long by 21 angstroms wide on every cycle of the double helix spiral. Looking back at the Fibonacci sequence above, you will find that 34 and 21 are Fibonacci numbers.[5]

The sequence and ratio seen throughout various forms of creation are not only aesthetically pleasing but serve a functional purpose as well. Sunflowers are the perfect example of this. Their seed pattern follows the rule of the Fibonacci Sequence. The pattern is beautiful, but beyond that, the pattern serves a specific purpose. Because the seeds follow the Fibonacci Sequence, space is optimized and shadowing of the seeds is decreased. This maximizes the amount of sunlight the flower receives and reiterates the appropriate naming of the sunflower. God isn't a God of coincidence. He is deliberate in everything He does, down to the pattern of sunflower seeds.

How Much More?

So much can be said by observation of nature through numbers and science. If plants and animals were created with such intricate and purposeful design, down to the exact incremental layout, how much more valuable is the intention we were created with? If He creates a single blade of grass that lives one day and dies the next, with such detail, how much more detail does He have planned out through us (Luke 12:28 ESV)?

How much more?

How much more value does our life hold than we tend to appraise it for?

How much more purpose do we have than we tend to believe?

How much more of the goodness of God's plan could we see if we only laid aside our own plans?

What would it look like if we lived our lives with our creation's purpose in mind? How would we spend our time?

We waste so much time worrying about the things of this world that we miss out on just how special God's plan for us is.

Jesus repeats the phrase "how much more" during His ministry to remind us of the value and purpose God created us in as His children. "Consider the ravens: they neither sow nor reap, they have neither storehouse nor barn, and yet God feeds them. Of how much more value are you than the birds" (Luke 12:22-24 ESV).

We don't need to worry about the details of this life. Our value in the sight of the Lord is so high that He has already worked out the details. This is not a prosperity gospel but rather a promise of Who we are created in.

We are created in the One who knows all.

Even when our heart leads us astray, God is greater (1 John 3:20 ESV). God sees what was before us and sees what is ahead of us. He knows our needs even when we do not. He sees purpose even when we cannot.

It never ceases to amaze me how people going through the most heartbreaking circumstances can lift their hands in worship and surrender their will fully in trust of God. A family

I walked alongside in my teenage years experienced the loss of their youngest son. I considered him a little brother but also a spiritual leader. In the last couple years of his life, he battled a rare cancer that took much of his physical strength but only solidified the magnitude of his spiritual strength. His tenacious love for the Lord in the middle of such great pain that took him from this world has won many hearts to Christ over the years. His maturity in his faith was beyond anyone else I have ever witnessed first-hand. He wrote in a journal about how he related to Paul, who said, "To live is Christ, and to die is gain" (1 Philippians 1:21 ESV). He spent his last few years on Earth truly living by waking up daily to live out his God-given purpose.

When he died, my heart ached for his sweet family. I knew they were hurting, but I will never forget what his mother said to me in the midst of her deepest grief. She said, "He was never ours." She shared what a gift it was to parent her son while he lived his life the way God intended.

He was never ours...

If only we could live our own life with this same intention. *My life is not mine...*

How much more of Jesus could we experience on this side of heaven if we spent our days as if they were never ours in the first place?

How much more?

The testimony of this family is forever etched on my heart. I am reminded that our time here is not only precious but filled with a greater purpose than we could ever imagine. Our impatience and selfish ambitions far too often get in the way and distract us from the joy God has to offer during this lifetime. When we can learn to lean in to His purpose, we are most fulfilled.

I didn't learn that lesson quickly and am still learning what

Coming Out Restored

it means to fully lean into His plan without interfering, but what I have learned so far is so intricately beautiful. Like the sunflower's seed pattern woven as intentionally as they are, God's intention in my life and His intention in yours is far more than meets the eye. When we offer ourselves as living sacrifices to the Greatest Love of our life, we get to see bits and pieces of His heaven here and now. As we wait with anticipation for the day of perfection when Christ returns, we can relish in what He is restoring us to - Imago Dei - the Image of God.

> Praise be to the God and Father of our Lord Jesus Christ! In his great mercy he has given us new birth into a living hope through the resurrection of Jesus Christ from the dead, and into an inheritance that can never perish, spoil or fade. This inheritance is kept in heaven for you, who through faith are shielded by God's power until the coming of the salvation that is ready to be revealed in the last time. In all this you greatly rejoice, though now for a little while you may have had to suffer grief in all kinds of trials. These have come so that the proven genuineness of your faith—of greater worth than gold, which perishes even though refined by fire—may result in praise, glory and honor when Jesus Christ is revealed. Though you have not seen him, you love him; and even though you do not see him now, you believe in him and are filled with an inexpressible and glorious joy, for you are receiving the end result of your faith, the salvation of your souls.
>
> — 1 Peter 1:3-9 ESV

Conclusion

I may be doing things out of order but I just finished writing the introduction and I am here now writing the conclusion. As I wrote and reread the last line of the introduction, I was hit with a wave of emotion. "From death to life, I am restored." Tears flowing down my face, I'm overwhelmed wondering, *why me?* Not in a self-deprecating kind of way.

Why me?

Why has God granted me this opportunity to be saved from myself and from a hell I deserved? I'm overcome with grace and mercy that overflows in abundance from the Almighty God. This is what an encounter with God feels like. It's overwhelming. It's emotional. And it's the most beautiful experience you could ever have. My prayer right now for you in whatever your circumstance is that you have an encounter such as this.

May God soften your heart where it needs to be softened.

May He speak to you in a way that you know He is undoubtedly for you and not against you.

May you feel the incomparable love of Christ.

May your life be changed in a way where you desire to never turn back to who you thought you once were.

May you be restored and redeemed by God, our good good Father.

May God reveal to you your true identity in Him. You are made in the image of the Almighty God. You are marked with the most incredible identity you could ever have - Imago Dei.

May you experience what it feels to know that you are a child of His, made in His perfect image, to reflect His likeness.

May you be overcome by the goodness of God.

And may you have a *"why me?"* moment.

If you've begun to encounter such a beautiful shift, my prayer and advice to you – don't quench the Holy Spirit. With open hands, ask God to quiet your mind and open your heart. Then, make note of what He is doing.

Before you close this book I want to reiterate the greatest truth I've come to realize. There is nothing, and I mean *nothing*, that compares to the love of Christ. My terrible habit of thinking I know best and awful track record of trying to do life my way has only proven me I don't do life well on my own. The truth is, I am nothing without Christ and nothing gives me more empowerment, peace, and joy than knowing that and choosing life God's way. The same is true for all of us and I can only pray that you will know that for yourself if you don't already. Blessings to you, my friend.

Notes

1. Into the Woods and Out of the Closet

1. "identity | Etymology, origin and meaning of identity by etymonline." n.d. Etymonline. Accessed October 21, 2023. https://www.etymonline.com/word/identity.
2. Merriam-Webster.com Dictionary, s.v. "truth," accessed July 29, 2024, https://www.merriam-webster.com/dictionary/truth.
3. Yuan, Christopher. 2018. *Holy Sexuality and the Gospel: Sex, Desire, and Relationships Shaped by God's Grand Story*. N.p.: Crown Publishing Group.
4. Keller, Timothy, and Kathy Keller. 2013. *The Meaning of Marriage: Facing the Complexities of Commitment with the Wisdom of God*. p 101.: Penguin Publishing Group.
5. Leaf, Dr. C. 2019. *The Perfect You: A Blueprint for Identity*. p52.: Baker Publishing Group.
6. Leaf, Dr. C. 2019. *The Perfect You: A Blueprint for Identity*. p 52-53.: Baker Publishing Group.

2. Sprouting

1. Leaf, Dr. C. 2019. *The Perfect You: A Blueprint for Identity*. p 33.: Baker Publishing Group.

3. Dry Lands

1. "Deconstruction Definition & Meaning." n.d. Merriam-Webster. Accessed November 30, 2023. https://www.merriam-webster.com/dictionary/deconstruction.
2. Davison, Amy. n.d. "84. Understanding Deconstruction: A Conversation with Alisa Childers." Mama Bear Apologetics. Accessed November 29, 2023. https://mamabearapologetics.com/mba084-deconstruction-alisa-childers/.
3. Graham, Billy, and Donna L. Toney. 2011. *Billy Graham in Quotes*. Edited by Franklin Graham and Donna L. Toney. p49.: Thomas Nelson.
4. Ruiter, Grace. n.d. "Advice for When You're Struggling with Faith." Faithward.org. Accessed December 4, 2023. https://www.faithward.org/advice-for-when-youre-struggling-with-faith/.

Notes

4. Fenceless Gardens

1. TerKeurst, Lysa. 2022. *Good Boundaries and Goodbyes: Loving Others Without Losing the Best of Who You Are*. p21: Thomas Nelson.
2. Haas, Melissa. 2018. *L.I.F.E. Recovery Guide for Spouses: A Workbook for Living in Freedom Everyday in Sexual Wholeness and Integrity*. Edited by Dr. Mark Laaser. p136: Independently Published.
3. TerKeurst, Lysa. 2022. *Good Boundaries and Goodbyes: Loving Others Without Losing the Best of Who You Are*. p45: Thomas Nelson.

7. A Wolf in Sheep's Clothing

1. Merriam-Webster.com Dictionary, s.v. "foothold," accessed July 29, 2024, https://www.merriam-webster.com/dictionary/foothold.
2. "Forgiveness Definition | What Is Forgiveness." n.d. Greater Good Science Center. Accessed February 17, 2024. https://greatergood.berkeley.edu/topic/forgiveness/definition.

9. Tree Stumps

1. Ritenbaugh, Richard T. 1995. "The Remnant." Church of the Great God. https://www.cgg.org/index.cfm/library/article/id/544/remnant.htm.
2. Miller, Philip. 2022. "The Fruitful Life of the Spirit." cslewisinstitute.org. https://www.cslewisinstitute.org/resources/the-fruitful-life-of-the-spirit/.

10. Seeing Sunflowers

1. O'Donnell, Amanda, Sarah Hepola, Rose Cahalan, Aisling Ayers, Peter Holley, Kristen Steenbeeke, Skip Hollandsworth, et al. 2023. "Texas Summer Gardening Is Brutal. These Two Native Species Don't Mind." Texas Monthly. https://www.texasmonthly.com/travel/texas-summer-gardening-tips-sunflowers-drought-zinnias/.
2. "Biology Of Sunflowers Uncovered | Nuseed Europe." 2022. Nuseed Global. https://nuseed.com/eu/biology-of-sunflowers-uncovered/.
3. Lacy, Chris. 2023. "YHWH: His Breath in Our Lungs. God's name sounds like breathing: YH... | by Chris Lacy | Medium." Chris Lacy. https://chrislacy1990.medium.com/yhwh-his-breath-in-our-lungs-21c2bc60571b.
4. Piacquadio, Andrea. n.d. "The Fibonacci Sequence – God's Design Pattern is Everywhere." Evidence To Believe. Accessed April 21, 2024. https://evidencetobelieve.com/the-fibonacci-sequence-gods-design-pattern/.

Notes

5. Choi, Jiwon, Agegnehu Atena, and Wondimu Tekalign. 2023. "The Most Irrational Number that Shows up Everywhere: The Golden Ratio." Scientific Research Publishing. https://www.scirp.org/journal/paperinformation?paperid=124651.

Acknowledgments

Thank you to my husband for your support, love, and willingness to grow with me. I'm grateful for your persistence, your ability to make me laugh when I don't want to, and for the fact that we made a really fun and cute kid.

Mom and Dad, thank you for loving me and praying for me always. I am blessed to have you as my parents. Please forgive me for the times I have not shown that and maybe forget those teenage years when I expressed the opposite.

To my prayer warriors, your gift of prayer means more to me than you will ever know. For the times I didn't want your prayers, thank you for not letting up. I humbly admit I needed them (and still do). My appreciation is beyond words.

Thank you to my writing coach, Adam Davis. Your prayers, knowledge, and support have truly been God-given. I don't know how you do it all, but I am grateful you made the time for me even if it meant sending your edits at 2 AM. Don't worry, my notifications were on silent.